Love in Translation

Also by Joss Wood

The Trouble with Little Secrets
Keep Your Enemies Close...
Hired for the Billionaire's Secret Son
A Nine-Month Deal with Her Husband

Visit the Author Profile page at Harlequin.com for more titles.

JOSS WOOD

L**O**VE
IN

TRANSLATION

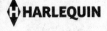

HARLEQUIN®

Recycling programs
for this product may
not exist in your area.

ISBN-13: 978-1-335-57488-6

Love in Translation

Copyright © 2024 by Joss Wood

Harlequin Enterprises ULC
22 Adelaide St. West, 41st Floor
Toronto, Ontario M5H 4E3, Canada
www.Harlequin.com

Printed in U.S.A.

To Vaughan, Rourke and Tess.
You three turn my world.

One

Four months had passed since her hot-mic incident went viral—the start of her downward spiral—but to Rheo Whitlock, it felt like yesterday.

It was obvious her boss didn't feel the same way.

Nicole's on-screen gaze was unflinching. Her boss was running short on sympathy. "You do realize you've been on medical leave for sixteen weeks now?" Nicole demanded.

Rheo's face flamed and she bit down on the inside of her cheek to keep from apologizing. Oh, she knew exactly how long she'd been stuck in this level of hell. She vividly remembered the day Nicole and the work-appointed psychologist suggested she take some time to get, in layman's terms, her shit together.

Admittedly, gathering said shit was taking longer than anticipated. Getting through the day was still a challenge—concentrating enough to finish any type of project was impossible, and emptiness accompanied her everywhere. Work-related burnout wasn't fun.

"When do you think you might be ready to return to work?"

And there it was, the question Rheo had been dreading since she got the email asking her to attend an online meeting with her manager earlier this morning. Next week? Next month? Six months? *Never?* Rheo didn't know, and couldn't guess, when she'd be mentally, and emotionally, ready to go back. And the only way to test whether she could handle a high-pressure situation requiring nerves of steel was to jump back into the job. She would either do what she'd once done best—real-time, on-the-spot interpreting—or she'd freeze. If she blanked, she'd embarrass herself, Nicole, her colleagues in the Spanish section, and her employer, the United Nations Interpretation Service. *Again.*

Oh, and there was also the chance of her causing an international incident. Hopefully, she'd stop short of starting World War III.

After the hot-mic incident, she would always be known as the interpreter who screwed up. During one of the most important General Assembly climate change debates in decades, she'd castigated political leaders for their inaction, thinking her mic was off.

The viral video triggered her steep fall from grace. Since just the thought of interpreting for high-level politicians or trade ministers again made her heart race and her throat close, Rheo suspected she wasn't anywhere near ready to go back. "Nicole, I'll get back to you with a date as soon as

I can." It wasn't the answer her boss wanted, but it was all she could give.

As soon as Nicole's face faded from her screen, Rheo leaned back in her chair and placed her bare feet on the corner of the desk, flayed and fried. Rolling her head to release the knots in her neck, she tipped her head and inspected the ceiling. An enormous spiderweb flowed from the top of the overlarge oil seascape to the corner of the molded ceiling.

She should do some cleaning, but she didn't have the energy.

Rheo wiggled and popped open the button of the denim shorts digging into her stomach. Maybe she should start cutting back on cheese. And wine. And chocolate. She'd picked up a few pounds and wasn't sure she'd fit into any of the sleek suits and pencil skirts she wore for work...

If she went back to work.

She so wanted to return, but she wasn't ready. Had she lost the skills she possessed before she, as her ex liked to say, screwed the pooch? Which she'd done extremely well, because Rheo never half-assed anything.

A planner and a perfectionist, she treated her life as a project to be micromanaged. Unlike her messy, frequently chaotic, and disorganized childhood, her adult life ran with the extreme efficiency of a Swiss clock. She had goals, objectives, deliverables, risks, and countermeasures and hit all her milestones with startling accuracy. Unfortunately, she'd also sabotaged her career with equal proficiency in the aftermath of the hot-mic incident.

In the days following that humiliation, her colleagues

picked up errors in her translations, *twice*. Another colleague caught her sobbing in the ladies' bathroom and gleefully told her coworkers she'd lost her edge—an accurate but, God, so humiliating observation. Then, as her faux pas hit the news and social media, garnering millions—*freakin' millions!*—of views, her brain short-circuited and her words disappeared while she translated for the Spanish finance minister during a high-level trade delegation.

All her words—she was fluent in Spanish, German, Italian, and French, and could converse in Portuguese and Romanian—went *poof.* One moment she could translate and speak what she'd heard while listening to the sentences that followed, and the next she couldn't ask for directions in any of the many languages she could speak.

Her phone beeped with a message, and Rheo pounced on it, hoping for a distraction. She wrinkled her nose when she saw Nicole's name on her grubby screen.

I'm being pressured by the higher-ups about finding a permanent replacement for you, Rheo. I've insisted on allowing you time to recover, but the max is six months. If you don't return to work in two months, you will be replaced.

Nicole didn't understand the concept of pussyfooting around.

Don't make me look for a replacement, Whitlock.

Rheo flipped her phone over, then over again. This wasn't the life she'd planned. Gilmartin, Washington—the town of outdoor adventures—wasn't where she should be living for any length of time.

Paddy, her grandmother, didn't know she was here, squatting in her vacation home without her permission. Neither did the rest of her family, for that matter. Her van-life-loving, adventurous parents, and her extended family all thought she was still happily ensconced at the UN. And because she was stingy with personal information, they believed she and Callum, the boyfriend none of them had met, were still together.

They had no idea the life she'd planned was a soggy mess.

Sitting here in this town she loathed, she felt six again, confused, disoriented, and alone.

Needing a distraction, Rheo moved across the room and sat on the built-in seat of the bay window, stretching her long legs. The road ended four houses down, and at the T-junction, one of the many extensive forests surrounding Gilmartin started. Through the thick tree trunks, she caught glimpses of the always impressive Columbia River glinting in the summer sun. Like so many other towns situated on the river, Gilmartin possessed old-time charm and was often described in travel brochures as quaint and quirky.

Nature lovers raved about this part of the country and gushed over the snow-capped mountains, the emerald-green lush and thick forests, fast-flowing rivers, and sparkling blue lakes. Just the kind of place that the rest of her family couldn't get enough of. But Rheo's heart ached for the sliver of Prospect Park she could see from her bedroom window and for her tiny windowless cubicle in the UN Plaza building.

Unless you experienced it for yourself, no one understood

the adrenaline of stepping into a UN interpretation booth. The booths overlooked the impressive rotunda of the General Assembly Hall. She was always conscious of the importance of the events playing out in the impressive room and in the smaller meeting rooms scattered throughout the building. Within those walls, she and her colleagues had to quickly and accurately translate decisions, discourse and opinions.

She wanted to rewind time and return to the normality of regular paychecks, the security of her apartment, and her regular but brief interactions with her neighbors. She wanted what was comfortable, expected, everything that was predictable and planned for. She'd lived the first thirteen years of her life in turmoil and chaos. Her parents loved the unexpected and unforeseeable, but Rheo hated the shifting sand under her feet.

Or, more accurately, the rickety wheels of their always-breaking-down van.

Crap, she couldn't get out of her head today. *Think about something else, Whitlock, stop marinating in self-pity. Do something, call someone.*

Despite spending her childhood summers here, she'd lost touch with the long-time residents of Gilmartin and had only made one friend since she'd arrived—Abi Curtis, the owner of the town's deli and coffee shop. She and Abi bonded over their love of good food, excellent books, their mutual distaste for exercise, and their imperviousness to the charms of the vast natural wilderness surrounding Gilmartin.

They were poles apart—Abi was a little scatterbrained, slightly disorganized, and loud, God, so loud—but they'd instantly connected. Despite only knowing her for a few months, Rheo could call her at four in the morning and, without quibbling, knew Abi would help her bury the body. How was it that she could connect with someone who was so unlike her, but Rheo couldn't relate to her own oh-so-different family? Strange.

Abi also possessed the uncanny ability to get Rheo out of her self-obsessed funk, so Rheo pulled up her name. Within a few seconds, Abi's gorgeous face filled her screen. Dark-haired and even darker-eyed, Abi was tall, buxom, and full-figured…super sexy.

Rheo took in the white wraparound top showing off Abi's canyon-like cleavage, and looked down at her own modest B-cup boobs. Sadly, there was no contest.

"You busy?" Rheo asked.

Abi turned her phone to show the mostly empty coffee shop and, beyond it, her deli. "We're between the breakfast and lunch rush, so I can talk. What are you up to?"

Rheo shrugged. "Sitting here, looking at the view. It's fucking gorgeous."

Abi hooted at her deadpan expression and flat monotone. When she stopped laughing, Abi insisted Rheo admit it was a beautiful day.

Meh.

Before her tenth birthday, she'd seen the geysers at Yellowstone Park, the Antelope and Bryce Canyons in Arizona and Utah, glaciers in Alaska, and sky-high redwoods in California. She'd been forced to visit wild places, hike trails, scramble up mountains, and paddle rivers. She'd promised herself she'd never live anywhere she was out of her element again. Yet, here she was, back in Gilmartin, surrounded by crapping nature. It wasn't part of the plan. Epic fail.

"I've seen too much of the great outdoors to get excited."

Abi, because she'd landed in Gilmartin via a bad kayaker boyfriend and a broken-down truck, didn't push the point. She leaned her hip against the counter and pushed a corkscrew curl behind her ear. "I still can't imagine you living in a camper van, Rhee."

"I was a kid and smaller," Rheo pointed out. "But, admittedly, when I hit puberty, it became more of a nightmare. Thin walls."

Abi pulled a face. "*Eeeww.* Listen, I'm free tonight. Should I bring a pizza over?"

"Sounds good."

Rheo watched as an older model SUV, one of those British ones, trundled down the road, its white body streaked with dust. It slowed as it approached the neat bungalow two doors up and then swung to park in front of Mrs. Redfern's pale gray house. That house was much more Rheo's own style than her grandmother's, actually. Paddy, in a fit of pique after her divorce, painted her ex-husband's overly large Victorian family home coral over forty years ago. Rheo had never known it to be anything but a shade of provocative pink.

"I need to talk to Paddy about painting this house a sensible color," she told Abi. "I love her, but, God Almighty, someone should've banned her from choosing paint. What's wrong with a sensible pale blue or cream?"

"Mmm, I see two problems with your statement. One,

your grandmother doesn't know you are living in her house, and having that conversation would be a good way of cluing her in."

Right. Good point.

"And even if Paddy agreed, and she never would, you'd also have to deal with the backlash from your neighbors and the town's residents. They'd stage a riot if the Pink House wasn't pink anymore," Abi said, then tipped her head to the side. "You aren't comfortable with nonconformity, are you?"

Well, no. Wasn't that obvious?

Until she hit college, she had been an outsider looking in, wondering when she'd feel at home in her life, in her skin. This time last year, she'd finally, *finally* arrived at a place in her life where she could breathe without restrictions, talk without being judged, where she was completely comfortable. She'd had a normal, not too good-looking, not too assured boyfriend, a great job, and a lovely apartment in the city she adored. Predictable, sure, but that was how she'd planned it. She'd finally acquired the life she'd dreamed of: steady, stable, and conventional. Her experience-chasing family members would call it unexciting, but unlike them, she didn't like rocking the boat.

She'd worked damn hard to find a safe harbor to moor in, sheltered from any storms, a place where she belonged.

Then life decided to be a tempestuous bitch and slapped her with a super typhoon.

Rheo watched the driver's door to the Land Rover open and a big boot hit the road, followed by the frayed cuff of well worn jeans. Her eyes slid up long legs and over a wide chest and tanned arms, and only two words rolled off her tongue. "Oh, *yum*."

"What?" Abi demanded.

Rheo turned her phone so Abi could watch the man open the back passenger door and pull a duffel and a laptop bag from behind the driver's seat. His overlong scruffy hair, a light brown interspersed with dark blond natural highlights, blew in the wind, and he impatiently pushed it off his face. A dirty-blond week-old beard covered his jaw and cheeks. The details of his face escaped her, but it was as rugged as the mountains in the distance. But who cared about his face when it was accompanied by *that* incredible body?

"Oh. My. God."

Rheo swung her phone back and grinned. "Hot, right?"

"So hot," Abi agreed. "Turn your phone around, I don't want to see you!"

Rheo flipped the camera again—sharing was caring—and inspected the neighborhood's latest visitor. He was tall and built. He sported the wide shoulders of an Olympic swimmer, and the muscles of his big arms strained the bands of his plain red T-shirt. His ancient jeans, faded to a soft dusty blue, clung to long muscled thighs, and his T-shirt skimmed a broad chest and flat stomach. He wasn't Rheo's type; even from a distance she sensed he was wild, untamable, and unpredictable. He was trouble with a capital T. In bold.

She liked her men urbane, controlled, stable, and steady. Men like that suited her life. The hottie outside was six-feet-plus of chaos.

"Do you think he's got those sexy hip muscles, the ones that make a V?" Abi asked, wistful.

"Yep. You do know that we are totally objectifying him, right?"

Abi made a *pfttt* sound, so Rheo didn't pull her phone, now resting on her knee, or her eyes off him.

He turned his head left, then right, looking for house numbers before walking *toward her house*. She sat statue still, rooted to her seat, hoping he'd notice her sitting in the window and then hoping he wouldn't. Ten yards, five, three…

"Is he heading your way?" Abi demanded.

Yep. Maybe.

He turned his head from his perusal of the street and looked left, and eyes the color of rain-soaked moss collided with hers through her open window. The smack of attraction made her sway, and air rushed from her lungs. His face was better than she expected, with a squarish jaw, strong brows, and a long nose. He was breath-stealingly good-looking.

And in that moment, the concept of instant attraction morphed from fantasy into reality.

It was shimmery…and scary.

Rheo's stomach flipped, and baby fireworks danced on her skin. All she could do was stare at him. He stopped on the sidewalk outside her house. For the first time in her staid—some would say boring—adult life, a life *she'd* created and loved, Rheo suspected she'd follow a man anywhere.

Rheo sighed as reality strolled in and sat its ass down. Of course, she wouldn't do anything of the sort. She was the least impulsive person she knew. She didn't make rash decisions, she made pro and con lists and did feasibility studies. All her relatives, except for Paddy, flew by the seat of their pants, but Rheo always considered all the consequences and chose the option with the least risk of things going wrong.

Sure, she could be a pain in the ass, but was never caught, as her parents so often were, with her pants down.

Except, of course, when she blew her life apart and abandoned her job, apartment, and perfect life. Except for then.

Rheo pulled a face, annoyed. He was a good-looking guy: so the hell what? Too much fresh mountain air was affecting her brain. She needed the exhaust fumes of a polluted city to get her thinking straight.

But that didn't stop her from scooting to the other side of the bay seat to continue watching his progress. His back view was as good as his front, and his ass in those soft jeans was exceptionally fine.

"What's happening? Why am I seeing fuzz?" Abi wailed.

Rheo flipped the camera back to look at Abi. "He's definitely coming here."

Abi's eyebrows shot up as the sound of the ancient doorbell drifted through the hall and into the study. "Do you know him? Why's he there?"

"No, and I don't know," Rheo told her. "Not even Paddy knows I'm here—"

"Something that's *so* going to blow up in your face," Abi informed her. Her friend took every opportunity she could to persuade her to come clean with her grandmother and the rest of her family. Rheo would when she felt ready and when she found the courage she needed to confess.

Paddy's doorbell made its about-to-die sound again and Rheo jumped. She stabbed her phone's screen and cut Abi off—oh, she'd pay for that later!—and hauled in some much-needed air. She had a stranger standing on her step…

One of the problems with being a semi-recluse for four months was that she'd grown unaccustomed to making small talk. She didn't know what to say or how to act. Rheo had never been great at chitchat, couldn't flirt, and was naturally shy, not helped by spending much of her childhood with only books for company.

Dear God, Whitlock! Just say hello and ask him how you can help!

Wiping her damp hands on the denim fabric covering her butt, Rheo walked into the spacious hallway. She took a deep breath—surprised that her heart could beat this fast—and pulled open the door.

"Hi? Um…can I help you?"

Those stunning eyes, flashing with intelligence, started at her bare feet and lazily climbed her body. He looked weirdly fascinated.

Rheo looked down. She'd "top dressed" to appear pro-fessional for her video call with Nicole. From the waist up she looked office-ready: a men's-style black button-down shirt, big gold earrings, and a funky copper and gold neck-lace. She'd added some light eye makeup and slicked on her favorite, only-for-special-occasions lipstick, YSL's Le Rouge, for some extra confidence. But below the waist, her style could only be described as scruffy. A ragged pair of denim shorts just covered her butt cheeks, and she'd left her flip-flops somewhere.

The corners of his lips lifted and her knees softened. She didn't think that was physically possible. Irritatingly, her synapses weren't firing too well either.

"Hey. I presume you're here to give me the key to this place?"

His accent matched his iconic British SUV: rough, deep, a little cut glass, a touch of lilt, a smidgeon of a burr. American enough to suggest he'd lived in this country for a while but Scottish enough to suggest his roots were buried in Celtic soil.

What did he say?

"Why would I give you a key?" she asked, puzzled.

"Because I've rented this place for the next few weeks?" He shifted his duffel bag to his other hand.

Das meinst du nicht im ernst?

"Why are you speaking German?"

She waved his question away. "Seriously?" she repeated her question in English. What was happening here?

"Carrie Whitlock told me I could find a key under the foot of the porch swing, but when I noticed you in the window, I assumed she arranged for you to meet me here to hand it over."

Puzzle pieces floated around her brain, but none of them slotted together. "How do you know Carrie?"

"We've been friends for years."

Friends, huh? And a pink pig just flew past.

He was the male equivalent of her lovely cousin: another

member of the tribe of golden people: at ease in their skin, innately confident, and blindingly self-assured. Bold, gorgeous, ripped.

And, like Carrie, he made Rheo feel like a hobbit.

"I'm into outdoor adventures, and I've wanted to visit this area for years. Carrie suggested I rent this house and explore the area until she can join me in two weeks. Her grandmother agreed. Apparently, she doesn't like the house empty for long stretches of time."

"Bullshit!" Rheo snapped. "The Pink House is locked up every winter."

He shrugged. "I'm just passing on what I was told. Carrie's grandmother is considering extending her overseas trip, and renting the house will give her additional funds."

Hold on a minute. Carrie knew Paddy was thinking of staying longer in Australia, but Rheo didn't? Rheo got Paddy's news first; Paddy confided in *her*, not Carrie. Why was she, Paddy's favorite grandchild, playing catch-up?

Pot, kettle, black, Whitlock. You're keeping some pretty big secrets yourself!

"Carrie also mentioned something about the rent helping with the cost of repairs, because old houses are a bitch to maintain," he said, still looking relaxed and unhurried. "I'm her first client, a guinea pig of sorts. If letting the place doesn't turn out to be a problem, she might rent it again instead of selling. So the pressure is on me."

He grinned, inviting Rheo to share the joke, but she couldn't. "Selling?" she whispered, aghast.

His words slapped her, hot and hard. Rheo hated Gilmartin, but she loved this house, and her best memories of her childhood and Paddy, the woman who loved and understood her best, the woman she didn't want to disappoint, rested within the walls of this building.

Rheo wanted nothing more than to call her grandmother and yell at her for considering such a drastic option and then beg her not to sell. But she couldn't because Paddy didn't know she was here…

She caught the curiosity in his mossy green eyes and, beneath it, interest and a hit of heat. Or was she imagining his attraction? She probably was; goddesses like her cousin were his jam.

The Pink House's new tenant was too much of a distraction, the reason Rheo couldn't think clearly. And, God, she needed time to think. Just ten minutes, even five. Time to get blood back to her brain and her heart to stop its Energizer-Bunny-on-speed bouncing.

So Rheo did the only thing she could think of and slammed the heavy wooden door in his flabbergasted face.

Two

"Hey!"

Rheo rested her forehead on the door and shivered as his deep voice rolled under the frame, through the cracks, and penetrated the wood. For the first time, goose bumps pebbled her skin and tiny fireworks exploded in her stomach. They'd just looked at each other, for God's sake!

Stop lusting and start thinking, dammit!

If he walked away, he'd contact Carrie and ask her why Rheo was living in the house he'd rented. The police would be called, and...*boom!*

If she told him her grandmother owned the house and Carrie was her cousin, he'd tell Carrie there was a mix-up and...*boom!*

Carrie would tell Paddy...

Big boom!

"I'm just going to call Carrie and get this sorted," he told her, his deep voice barely muffled by the thick door.

Carrie, according to her Instagram account, was live-streaming her hike to the summit of an active volcano—*typical*—and Rheo doubted she'd answer his call. But she might, so Rheo yanked the door open and snatched his phone.

"What the hell?" he demanded, looking from his empty hand to hers.

"Don't call her. We can sort this out," Rheo said, hating the note of panic in her voice.

He plucked his phone back. "Who *are* you? And why am I discussing any of this with you?"

His expression hardened, and suspicion flared in his eyes. Damn, she'd run out of choices.

"I'm Rheo Whitlock, Carrie's my cousin, and our grand-mother, Paddy, owns this place."

"Rheo…" He rolled her name over his tongue and an-other flash of lust smacked her. *Oh, for God's sake!*

Rheo sucked in some much-needed air. "Who did you say you are?"

His lips lifted in a sexy half smile. "I didn't, but I'm Fletcher Wright. Fletch to my friends."

It was a good name, a strong name, but not one she recog-nized. He knew Carrie and he enjoyed outdoor pursuits, so he was probably part of her making-adventure-and-travel-documentaries world.

"Producer, director, or sound guy?"

Amusement flickered in his eyes, turning them a shade lighter. "I've done all of the above before."

It wasn't an explanation, but his occupation didn't matter. And although he'd been patient up to this point, he had to be wondering why she hadn't invited him into the house he'd rented.

He lifted his duffel bag—it looked heavy—and glanced at his bells-and-whistles watch. Rheo caught the flicker of impatience on his tired face. Thick blue stripes under his eyes suggested exhaustion, and despite his bulk, he looked to be a few pounds underweight. It was obvious he needed a week of solid sleep and decent meals.

But what he needed wasn't important—she couldn't afford to lose focus. She should invite him inside, but she couldn't, not yet. If she let Fletcher Wright walk into the house, his presence would change her life in ways she hadn't anticipated or planned for.

Her life was plenty complicated already, thanks very much.

"So, just to be clear…you are renting this house?" she asked.

Maybe she could find a solution to her quandary in the next thirty seconds.

Irritation flickered in his eyes at her question, but he nodded his response.

"For how long?"

"I'm not sure yet, but a minimum of three weeks. I have the option to extend the lease if I want to."

Three weeks? Holy shit! That long?

"You mentioned something about Carrie coming back?" she asked, hoping she'd misunderstood him. She couldn't cope with Captivating Carrie right now. "When?"

"She said she'd be here in two weeks. We intend to kayak the Little White Salmon together."

Despite her lack of interest in anything outdoorsy, Rheo knew the Little White Salmon was a world-famous kayaking run not far from here, offering incredible rapids...*if* you possessed the skills to attempt it. Competent Carrie did.

"We're also going to do some trail running, some soloing," Fletcher added.

Soloing was shorthand for rope-free climbing, and Rheo pulled a why-would-you-want-to-do-that face.

He grinned. "Which one don't you like? Trail running or climbing?"

Rheo waved her hand in the direction of Mount Hood. "All of it. Getting sweaty and dirty is not my idea of fun."

He leaned his big shoulder into the wall next to the front door and examined her face, his expression more intense than before. "I remember Carrie mentioning you. You have an important job in the city, and you work incessantly, right?"

He made it sound like work was all she did...

To be fair, he wasn't wrong. She did work long hours. She heard the questions he was too polite to ask out loud—*Jesus, how can you live like that? Don't you feel like a rat on a wheel?*—and sighed. Compared to her van-life-loving parents and the wildly adventurous, sexy, and charismatic presenter/adventurer/influencer Carrie, Rheo's life sounded dreary. But it was her life, her choice, and she didn't need to be constantly moving or climbing mountains or swimming with sharks to be content.

A good book and a glass of wine worked for her.

Everyone in her family, except for Paddy, felt the need to try to save her from her mindless existence—*For God's sake, live a little more! You need more stamps in your passport, Rheo! Do you even own a passport, Rheo?*—so she kept her interactions with them to a minimum, restricting their communications to a monthly email, and a call every two weeks for her to catch up on their adventures and for her parents to sigh when they heard her life was the exactly the same as last month and the month before. If they were in the same area, they sometimes met up to celebrate birthdays, Thanksgiving, and Christmas. If teeth-pulling conversation could be called celebrating.

And that was exactly why they'd be assuming now, that she still lived in the city and worked at the UN. They didn't know her career was in tatters or that she was fighting to find her way back to who she was before.

"It's a gorgeous house and bigger than I realized," Fletcher said, looking past her into the hall.

And it was the house he'd paid to lease. He had the right to be here; she didn't. Theoretically, she should pack up and ship out. But where would she go? Abi would let her sleep on her couch for a night or two, but Rheo was allergic to sharing her living space with anyone…which was the primary reason Callum had dumped her last year. He'd wanted them to move in together, but Rheo believed the three nights a week he slept over was two too many.

But the Pink House was way bigger than her apartment and definitely big enough to house two people who wanted, or needed, to live separate lives. Would Fletcher let her stay for a little while, just long enough to make a new plan? And if he did, would he also agree to keep her presence in Gilmartin a secret until she figured out what to do, where to go, and how to wiggle out of her self-created predicament?

She knew what she should do—bite the bullet and tell Paddy, and her parents, how she'd screwed up—but if she could get away with keeping her goat rodeo shit show under wraps, she would.

Pride might come before a fall, but at least she didn't have that far to drop.

Rheo rubbed the back of her neck. Okay, even if she managed to persuade Fletcher to share the house, how would she cope with living with him? He couldn't be ignored: he was a big guy and took up space. He exuded capability and charisma, the kind people noticed when walking into a room. It often happened at the UN. If one looked past the head honcho leading political delegations, there was someone at the back of the retinue not saying much, but when he (or she) did, people listened. And responded. Immediately. The power behind the mouthpiece, the true leader.

Fletcher was the same. Whether he meant to or not, knew it or not, he commanded attention.

He was also the first man who'd literally made her feel *exhilarated*. Dammit. Was this what her parents experienced when they scaled a rock face? What Carrie felt when she dived with white sharks or bungee-jumped off the bridge over Victoria Falls? All shaky and shivery and shiny? If yes, then Rheo didn't care for it. She liked stability in her emotions as well as her life, thank you very much.

Rheo watched old Mrs. Nicolson walk by, her head swiveling at the strange man standing on her doorstep. Rheo jerked her chin, gesturing for Fletcher to come inside.

He dropped his duffel bag to the black-and-white tiled floor and lowered his laptop case to rest on his bag, his attention caught by an oversized, colorful, but unsettling painting on the opposite wall. Paddy was convinced it was a work by Georgia O'Keeffe, one of her flower paintings, but Rheo thought it was porn adjacent and wished she'd take it down.

Fletcher asked to use the bathroom, and Rheo directed him to the small one behind the stairs. The door clicked shut, and Rheo ran her fingertips over her forehead, conscious of her pounding head. Her meeting with Nicole had left her drained, and having a sexy stranger drop onto her doorstep with the intention of staying knocked her off-balance.

Think, Rheo!

If she sent him away, he would call Carrie, and within thirty minutes, her phone would blow up with calls and messages from her family.

She couldn't tell them she'd failed. How would she explain her life was a mess and she was consumed by uncertainty? Oh, they weren't horrible people, they could be fun and great company, but she couldn't handle any *Come down to earth with a bump, haven't you?* comments.

Look, she didn't blame them; there had been a few times when she'd been pretty vociferous while expressing her scorn for their adventurous, nomadic lifestyles. She'd reprimanded her father for demanding to see Paddy's will, told Carrie she was insanely careless for visiting volatile Kashmir, and rolled her eyes at her mom's devotion to homeopathic medicines when an old-fashioned antibiotic would make her better quicker. It was human to gloat.

Carrie, who'd never met a secret she didn't spill, would tell Paddy that Rheo was staying at the Pink House, and an intense interrogation from her grandmother would commence. Her grandmother was many things—sensibly adventurous, soulful, intelligent, and shrewd—but she did not suffer fools, and she wasn't, and never had been, warm and fuzzy.

After Rheo explained she'd screwed up and bolted to Gilmartin, Paddy, always straightforward, wouldn't hesitate to wade in. After roasting her for using the house without permission, she'd drop a few conversational nuclear bombs in a withering tone.

I didn't raise you to wallow in self-pity, Rheo.

I expect you to admit your mistakes and face your problems. I am annoyed, and insulted, by your lack of action.

Hand-wringing wasn't Paddy's style.

Rheo tasted panic and her throat tightened. She wasn't nearly strong enough to deal with Paddy's take-no-prisoners commentary on her fucked-up life, not just yet.

Possibly not ever.

She needed a plan and another place to live. Unfortunately, that meant letting Fletcher Wright invade her privacy, upset her equilibrium, invigorate her libido, and move in. What other choice did she have?

Fuck all.

But would he let her stay?

Rheo lifted her head as Fletcher crossed the hallway to

where she stood. She clocked his confusion and a hint of disquiet. His sandy brows pulled together, and he gestured to the impressive front door. His movement drew attention to an intricate tattoo on the underside of his right arm, something arty and finely drawn. An ancient Greek sprite or a Roman goddess? She needed to inspect it up close to make sure.

"I'm not an idiot. I know you're living here."

Rheo wrinkled her nose and tipped her head, waiting for him to speak again. There was no point denying it.

"If Carrie was aware, she would've told me. You're keeping it a secret, for some reason, from them. How am I doing so far?"

"Pretty good."

"Where would you go if you left here?" Fletch asked.

Rheo spread her hands out. "I don't know. I've been trying to figure that out."

"It's a huge house and we can share it until you figure that out. But if you're uncomfortable doing that, I can book into a hotel, it's not a problem."

"I can't expect you to do that. You're paying to be here," she replied. Even if she could bypass her conscience to let him pay and leave, there was another problem. "I doubt you'd find a place to stay. Gilmartin is wildly popular during spring and summer, and hotel rooms are always hard to find. Besides, *I* should be moving out, not you," Rheo added, knowing she sounded glum.

His smile was more reassuring than she deserved. "As I said, it's a big place and I don't mind sharing. But if at any point you're unhappy about me staying in the house, I'll return to Portland. It's not a big deal," he told her, his words gentler than she expected.

That would require explanations to Carrie, who would… *blah, blah, blah*. Rheo rubbed her fingers across her forehead. *Les carottes sont cuites!* Either way, her carrots were cooked.

She snuck another look at him and a ripple of panic ran up her spine. Oh, he didn't scare her, he wouldn't hurt her, but her reaction to him terrified her. On meeting him, she'd stepped into an unstable bucket floating on a tempestuous ocean, and scariest of all, she *liked* this out-of-control feeling. All shaky and flaky and…yeah, weird.

She *was* weird. As Carrie often reminded her.

"But are *you* okay with me staying? Just until I get some of my ducks in a row?" she asked. *Hah!* Currently, her ducks were either stoned or drunk and she'd lost one or two.

One big shoulder lifted and dropped. "Sure, it's not a big deal."

Thank God.

"Thank you *so* much. I'll be gone before Carrie gets here. And I'll stay out of your way," Rheo added.

"We're just friends," Fletcher informed her. So he and the glamorous oh-so-confident Carrie weren't involved! *Whoot!* She didn't question why elation drifted through her.

"Thank you," Rheo told him, rocking on her heels.

He'd given her a massive gift, the gift of time, and she was grateful. Now she needed to use it. She couldn't mess around or procrastinate anymore. Her sole objective was to start untangling her messy life.

"Is that your grandmother?"

Rheo followed his gaze to the large silver-framed photo of her grandmother on the hall table. She smiled. "Yep, that's Paddy Whitlock, the one and only."

Thank God. The world couldn't cope with two of the same type.

Fletcher looked at the painting, lifted his eyebrows, and rested his hands on his hips. "Carrie's told me a little about her over the years."

"Like what?"

"I remember her saying that she treated Gilmartin as her fiefdom for more than fifty years. She had three sons, but the oldest one died in his...midtwenties."

Rheo nodded. "She's currently exploring Australia before she gets old." Paddy was moving from luxury accommodation to luxury accommodation, taking in the sights along the way. It was, in Rheo's mind, a sensible way to explore the world.

"She's in her eighties, right? Isn't she already old?"

Rheo laughed, enjoying him. "Don't ever say those words to her face. She will rip you apart. What else did Carrie tell you about Paddy?"

How many family secrets had her blabby cousin shared with Fletcher? Rheo particularly wanted to know what Carrie had said about her.

Actually, knowing how dismissive Carrie could be about her "boring" life and career, maybe she didn't.

"Ah...let me think. Paddy divorced her extremely rich husband and vowed she would never remarry."

"Their divorce was Gilmartin's great scandal of the summer of sixty-five, partly because they got divorced, mostly because she got the Whitlock family home in the settlement. She celebrated by opening this house up to anyone who caught her fancy. Every summer, she returned to the Pink House, and her parties became the stuff of legend. Some summers she hosted visitors for weeks or months on end," Rheo said.

And many visitors, male and frequently married, shared Paddy's bed. (Gilmartin residents still spoke of the spring, fall, and summer scandals of '67, '73, and '81). Paddy's love life was none of Rheo's business, and she didn't care about her lovers. Paddy was simply her grandmother, always welcoming and accepting. Paddy showed Rheo love by handing her a pile of books and allowing her to fall into the world between the pages. Paddy never made her take long hikes, nor did she expect Rheo to spend her time kayaking or climbing. Paddy allowed her to just *be*.

Her grandmother spoke French and Italian and encouraged Rheo to study other languages. She also nagged her to talk and engage with people, reminding Rheo she would never find her tribe if she didn't show people who she was. It was a lesson she had yet to master.

But points to her for finding Abi at one of the darkest times in her life. Abi, without much effort, slid into Rheo's life and under her skin, and their friendship was easy.

Rheo looked into her grandmother's blue eyes, eyes she'd inherited, and dropped her head in a small nod. *Point taken, Paddy.*

Fletcher shuffled behind her, and Rheo imagined Paddy's cutting comments about her lack of hospitality. She should take him to his room or give him a tour of the house. Paddy loved showing off her house, pointing out its handcrafted staircase, the handmade stained-glass windows, the views of the river and forests, and the mountains in the distance.

"I'll show you to the guest bedroom." Rheo nodded to his duffel bag. "Do you want to grab your stuff?"

"Tell me where to go and where to find linens and stuff. I can make the bed and sort myself out," Fletcher told her.

By Paddy's decree, the guest rooms, pristine and perfect, were always ready and required no fussing. But Rheo could've done with time to prepare for Fletcher's unexpected arrival. She planned, wrote lists, and wasn't an embrace-the-moment type of girl. She needed time, and lots of it, to adjust. And that was why, four months later, she hadn't come to terms with all the changes in her life.

How was she expected to handle her fierce, highly flammable attraction to this man?

"You won't need to feed, water, or entertain me, and I'll try and stay out of your way as much as possible," Fletcher said, following her.

Oh God, her hosting skills were so rusty! He was the tenant, she the temporarily homeless squatter.

"And I don't want to interrupt your work," he told her as they hit the first-floor landing.

Her work? What work? She turned to face him, frowning.

He gestured to her clothes. "Judging by your outfit, I assume you work online. You know, professional on top…"

"*Oh!* I had a meeting with my boss earlier."

"So, you *do* work?"

She wished. "I'm on sabbatical." Fletcher cocked his head, waiting for more. "I'm a simultaneous interpreter."

Wow. She never used big words to explain her job, but she wanted to impress him. *Pathetic.*

He scratched his head and looked confused. He looked kind of adorable. In a way that a ten-foot grizzly could look cuddly.

"I understand the words, but I'm not sure I get the concept."

"I'm a translator at the United Nations. I translate and speak in real time, facilitating communication between parties who speak different languages."

She heard the pride in her words, then felt shame on their heels. She'd jeopardized a job she loved, then made mistake after mistake.

Fletcher looked interested, so she continued. "Interpreters and translators are the lifeblood of the United Nations. Our linguistic skills put everyone on the same page. We facilitate communication and make the world a safer place. World leaders place their words in our hands, trusting we'll accurately get their messages across. It's a huge responsibility."

Heat hit her cheeks, and Rheo silently cursed, wishing she hadn't climbed onto her soapbox. He'd asked what she did, not for a dissertation about the importance of her job. It was easy to imagine Carrie rolling on the floor, laughing at Rheo's lack of cool. Rheo waited for Fletcher's response, her stomach in a knot.

"That's seriously impressive."

God, when had someone last looked at her like she was smart, remarkable...extraordinary? When had she last felt *seen*?

She'd trained herself to believe being alone was fine, desirable even, but his comment pierced her armor of self-sufficiency, a brief reminder of how wonderful it was to be admired, even appreciated.

Paddy, who never needed anyone's validation, would mock her for being weak enough to care how other people saw her. But Rheo sometimes—*most times*—did. She'd been forced into being emotionally self-sufficient at a young age, but she still hadn't gotten the hang of it.

Disconcerted by her attraction to Fletch, physical and now mental, Rheo opened the door to the guest room and walked inside, enjoying the cool, navy-and-white color scheme and the clean lines of the nonfussy furniture. The room suited Fletcher, who seemed like a no-frills type of guy.

He dropped his duffel bag to the floor and placed his laptop case on the surface of the wooden desk sitting under the wide sash windows. He took in the view of the forest and mountains in the distance, but she kept her eyes on him.

Her view was much better.

He was an action man, not handsome enough to be on magazine covers, but his vitality would turn heads. Interesting, attractive, magnetic...all those adjectives applied. As they did to her cousin. He and Carrie were ridiculously alike, both blond, beautiful, and bold.

But Rheo accepted his statement about there being nothing more than friendship between them. A good thing, because she couldn't think of anything worse than snacking on Carrie's leftovers.

Nothing would happen with Fletcher Wright. Life was complicated, and Rheo was too much of an emotional train wreck to think about sleeping with her new housemate.

You met him a short while ago, Whitlock, and you're already thinking about jumping him?

Who are *you?*

"I think you'll be comfortable in here," Rheo said, heading for the door to put some distance between them. The normally spacious room seemed small, and Rheo sensed the walls closing in on her.

"Thanks."

She couldn't help it, she just needed to check one more time. "And if Carrie phones or contacts you, you won't—"

His eyes narrowed and Rheo caught his irritation, a smidgen of anger. Standing in his line of fire wouldn't be a fun experience.

"I've already said that I won't tell Carrie you're here," he stated, his voice colder than before. "But I won't lie to her if she asks."

Okay, message received. Loud and clear. "Thank you."

Rheo lifted her bare foot to rub it against the back of her calf. He'd given her two weeks to sort out her life. Maybe a shorter deadline was exactly what she needed—it allowed her no time to brood or overanalyze. She needed to make a plan and put it into action. She could do it, she *would* do it...

Mostly because she didn't have a choice *but* to do it.

God, life could be such a temperamental bitch on occasion.

Fletcher turned and slid his hands into the back pockets of his jeans, pulling his T-shirt tight against his broad chest. His biceps stretched his sleeves. Desire, hot and sparkly, skittered along her skin.

"But I need you to do something for me." His eyes, now a deeper, bolder green, drilled into hers and pinned her to the spot.

She pulled in some air, and disappointment rippled through her. They'd made a deal and he was backtracking, reopening negotiations. What would he demand to keep her secrets? Man, she prayed he didn't ask her for something sleazy; she'd hate it if his pretty packaging concealed a jerk.

His eyes lightened and she caught a hint of a dimple in his stubble-covered cheek. His smile combined mischief and sex, and she couldn't imagine saying no to him—*ever*. Strange, because she always took her time to figure out her answer. And it was seldom yes.

Electricity arced, Rheo's body hummed, and she suspected the paint on the walls was starting to blister. "Um… okay. What?"

Fletcher took his time answering her. "Coffee."

Coffee? How could he be thinking about coffee?

"A cup of coffee, two sugars, would hit the spot."

Seriously?

Fletcher raised his eyebrows, and she noticed the naughty twinkle in his eyes. He was messing with her.

She expected irritation, but laughter bubbled up her throat. Carrie was just as confident, but *her* confidence made

Rheo feel less than, insignificant. His didn't. But, like her cousin, Fletcher had no issues asking for what he wanted, whether it was coffee or sex.

He definitely wanted coffee, but…

Did that mean sex was off the table? She'd met him just a half hour ago, but it seemed longer, as if he'd been part of her life for years rather than minutes. She felt comfortable with him, like she could grab his hand if she needed someone to steady her.

Madness. Her imagination was running away with her. She saved herself. Always had, always would.

But coffee…

Yeah, she could make him coffee. If her now completely melted brain remembered how.

Three

Fletch watched Rheo's round, delicious-looking ass until she was out of sight, and then blew air into his cheeks. He needed a moment to regroup. He was in Gilmartin, an area he'd always wanted to visit, in Carrie's grandmother's house. A house that wasn't, as assumed, unoccupied.

Fact: Carrie's cousin was living here, and Carrie didn't know.

Fact: Rheo was hot and he wanted her.

Yeah, they had chemistry in spades; it crackled and snapped, but nothing *like that* would happen with Rheo Whitlock. Fletch scrubbed his face. *Jesus Christ.* His fierce, immediate attraction to Carrie's prickly, pretty cousin was a ball ache he didn't need. If he was smart, he'd turn around, retrace his steps, and head back to Portland, his current base. Chances of him doing that? Roughly the same as him getting pregnant.

By immaculate conception.

Gilmartin, brimming with all the things he loved to do the most, intrigued him, and the Pink House was interesting and spacious. Unfortunately, his new housemate was a tiny meteor strike in human form. Earlier, he'd clocked her triangular, gamine face through the open bay window, and his mouth watered. Then she opened the door, and it took all his willpower not to drop to his knees.

She wasn't conventionally pretty but, God, she packed a punch. Her long hair was rope-thick, as brown as deep, rich, untreated Nepali coffee beans, and her pale skin reminded him of the champagne-colored bubble coral he'd seen diving a reef in the Philippines. He'd had to remind himself not to stare at her shapely legs in those denim cutoffs.

Her eyes, a startling, crystal-clear blue, made his brains leak from his ears. He hadn't felt this instinctive I-want-to-take-her-to-bed-immediately reaction to any woman since... well, forever. Before and after his expeditions—because he was a guy and not a monk—he'd taken what he could get: one-night stands, casual encounters, hookups with old friends. He was excellent at walking away. His reaction to Rheo was unusual; he was a little out of breath, a lot horny.

Fletch pulled in a breath, held it, released it in a long stream and rolled his shoulders. He was hot for his new housemate, and he'd agreed to keep her presence in the house, in this town, a secret.

You've been in town an hour, Wright. Excellent work.

His phone rang and Fletch scowled at the ceiling. He hated being constantly connected and available. He explored Earth's wild places because they were *wild*. There was so much to learn about the natural world, and himself, and he suffered extreme deprivations to gain that knowledge. Not always having a phone tucked into his back pocket was the biggest perk of his job.

He squinted at the screen and frowned. He'd made the mistake of telling Seb Michaels, the doctor on his expeditions and his closest friend, that he felt tired and unenergetic. Seb had insisted on giving him a thorough checkup. The ghoul drew blood and ordered a barrage of blood tests. Since Seb was calling from his office—Fletch recognized the old anatomical sketches on the wall behind him—he figured his results were back.

Feeling anxious—blood tests always made his neuroses kick in—Fletch sat on the edge of the big bed and swiped his screen to answer the video call. He frowned at Seb's muted greeting and far too serious expression.

"Your iron, folic acid, and magnesium levels are low. We can increase them by putting you on a good multivitamin."

Well, that sounded easy enough.

"Great. I'm thinking about a quickish solo trip to the Danakil Depression after I leave Gilmartin."

The area in the northeast corner of Ethiopia, often called the gateway to hell, was one of only four living lava lakes in the world. One of the hottest places on the planet and somewhere he longed to visit. When he returned, he'd start planning his next expedition—he was considering hiking, rafting, and skiing Alaska's most rugged wilderness, a five-thousand-mile route of mostly unexplored territory. Or climbing ten of the world's highest peaks. There was so much to do and see, and so little time.

Seb shook his head. "I'm not done, Fletch."

Fear tiptoed up his spine. Fletch was, routinely, a calm person and never overreacted. It was necessary because, in his line of work, if you panicked, you died. But when it came to his health, his legendary composure evaporated. Did he have cancer? Motor neuron disease? ALS? His stomach knotted.

As a teenager, he'd spent a year moving from his bed to the couch, mostly housebound and unable to do much more than lift the remote control. After leading such an active life for the past twenty years, he couldn't go back to that. The inactivity would kill him long before any disease did.

"What's wrong with me, Seb?" he demanded, annoyed to hear the tremor in his voice. His fears about getting sick again, and his medical history, were closely guarded secrets, and Seb—both doctor and best friend—was the only one he'd told.

"You're suffering from physical exhaustion, Fletch."

"CFS?" he demanded. At fifteen, he'd had strep throat, then rheumatic fever, and for the next nine months suffered from chronic fatigue syndrome. All he wanted to do, *could* do, was sleep. Exhaustion, dizziness, muscle and joint pain were all he remembered from that year.

People feared spiders and flying, his monster under the bed was being confined, being made to sit and stay.

"No, just run of the mill, normal tiredness."

Oh. Right.

"I've suggested that you take a break, and now I'm insisting," Seb stated in his scary doctor voice. His expression also suggested Fletch shouldn't argue. "One of the reasons we work well together is because I don't overreact and I'm not overly cautious. I trust you to know the limits of your own body, what you can and can't endure."

Seb, like him, wasn't a fusser, so when he looked stern and sounded resolute, Fletch had no choice but to listen.

"Your body needs a proper break, Fletch. You've had two bouts of malaria in three years. You've just recovered from a bout of pneumonia that was worse than you'll admit. You've had septicemia and frostbite. You've recovered from all of them and, I admit, you've recovered well."

There was a damn big *but* in there somewhere.

"But—"

There it was.

"—I insist you take a three-month break. You need to switch off. I don't want you doing any physical training. And I sure as hell do not want you going to the Danakil Depression."

Yeah, not happening. Nobody told him where he could and couldn't go. He'd made that unbreakable promise to himself when he was a teenager, and it was sacrosanct.

"And do not let Mick and Sam tempt you into joining them on one of their endurance hikes or runs," Seb told him.

Mick and Sam were nephews of their cameraman, Louie, who he'd met at a cookout a couple of summers ago. When Louie heard he was heading to Gilmartin, he'd told Mick and Sam—who owned a company that provided customers with outdoor experiences—to expect him to pop in. They'd already emailed him their company brochure and told him they could mix and match his adventures.

"I'm fine, Seb. And you know I can't afford to take so much time off or to stop training. I'm scheduled to be in Gilmartin for three weeks, and then I'll head to Ethiopia for a week. A you know, an expedition takes months to plan, and I hate delays."

Seb's expression remained stern and unyielding. "You seem to be forgetting you won't be able to get cover for any future expeditions without the certificate of health your insurers require from me. Without insurance, you won't get any sponsorship, and the producers of your documentaries won't touch you."

Fletch didn't need him to draw him a picture. "And you won't sign off unless I take a break? That's blackmail, Seb!"

Seb's bulldogged expression didn't change. "You say potato…"

Fletch glared at his oldest friend. "C'mon, Seb, you're going overboard. Can't we compromise on me taking three weeks off?"

"Uh…let me think…" Seb briefly looked away. "*No. Three months.* Or, if you prefer, we can make it four."

Right, he'd hit the line in Seb's sand. His friend wasn't going to budge, and there was no point in arguing with him any longer, so he cut the call. *Shit.* Tossing his phone from hand to hand, he considered firing Seb and hiring another doctor who'd greenlight him.

Shame washed over him. He was being a self-centered, spoiled prick. Seb had accompanied him on his last three expeditions and saved his life once. And—Fletcher was reluctant to admit this—Seb had a point. He was tired, mentally and physically.

But the thought of doing nothing for three months made his lungs constrict. When he'd recovered from CFS, he'd vowed to fill every moment living and not lying around. Back in Aberdeen, he'd sworn he'd delve into the world, discover every hidden nook and cranny, and he'd push himself, mentally and physically, to his limits. Every expedition he completed, every new stamp in his passport, visiting a strange town or place, was a victory against his past limitations. Unfortunately, his body was paying the price for his quest for adventure. He felt sluggish, and he wasn't sleeping properly.

Fletch shoved his fingers into his hair, frustrated. He expected to be caught flat-footed in mangrove swamps and on glaciers, in sandstorms and blizzards—places where nature flexed her muscles—but he objected to feeling disconcerted and off-balance in an old house in a small town in Washington State.

What was that old John Lennon quote, something about life happening when you were busy making other plans? Driving into Gilmartin earlier, Fletch had congratulated himself on his decision to visit this stunningly beautiful area. Three weeks of hiking, kayaking, and climbing—that was his ideal vacation. Having Carrie join him was a no-brainer. Her love of the outdoors, knowledge of the area, and their lack of chemistry made her the perfect companion.

No fuss, no drama.

But then he found Rheo.

And during their brief introduction, he'd discovered she hated all the things he loved and kept secrets from her family.

Other questions buzzed, as unrelenting as midges enjoying a warm summer evening in the Scottish Highlands. How many languages did she speak? Why was she taking a sabbatical? Why was he so bloody intrigued by her?

Irritated by Seb's pronouncement, Carrie's delayed arrival, and his unwelcome attraction to Rheo, Fletch walked over to the wide windows. Despite having stood on the summit of some of the world's highest mountains, watching the northern lights dance across the sky, and witnessing the fierce fury of an African thunderstorm, this view made his soul sigh with appreciation.

The deep, mysterious green of the forest contrasted beautifully with the blinding white snow on the upper reaches of Mount Hood. The sky was such a thick blue, dense enough to push his fist through it. The blue lakes glinted in the summer sun.

Man, he couldn't wait to get out there. Nature, somehow, always managed to soothe his soul, to smooth away his jagged edges, to give him a little perspective. He'd wake up to that view every morning for the next few weeks. A soft, warm breeze wafted into the room, tinged with a hint of roses and wildflowers and sweet, hot summer air.

"God, amazing," he muttered.

"Glad you like it." Rheo stood next to the bed, a pile of soft-looking towels in her hands.

She smiled, and his heart flip-flopped around his chest like a hooked rainbow trout.

She gestured to the door to her right. "There's a small en suite bathroom through there. It's not big, but it's got everything you need."

He nodded his thanks. He spent most of his year in cramped tents, and an en suite bathroom was an unexpected luxury. As was the wide bed, roomy enough for his long frame. At six four, his feet often hung off the ends of hotel beds, and he appreciated one he could stretch out in.

"The kitchen is downstairs to your right. Help yourself to coffee or anything in the fridge."

Fletch suspected Rheo was running through a mental checklist, trying to remember how to be a good hostess.

"There's a sitting room as well, with a TV."

Yeah, he wasn't a big TV watcher; he preferred to read. He'd caught a glimpse of an old-fashioned library earlier, complete with ceiling-high shelves stacked with books and ladders to reach the top. Would there be any books detailing long-ago expeditions?

"Can I use the library?"

Rheo looked at him as if he'd asked whether aliens were on the roof. "Of course you can. It's a *library*, the books are supposed to be read."

He'd visited houses where libraries were just for show, where books—special editions and collector's pieces—were seldom handled, sometimes never touched. No matter the cost or how rare, if he bought a book for his collection, he always read it. Oftentimes, he read it again.

"Thank you."

She pushed a tendril of thick hair behind her ear and nodded. "Sure. Um—" Her eyes landed on the bed, and a bright splash of pink hit her cheekbones.

Her eyes met his and skittered away. When she spoke again, her words tumbled over each other. "I'll leave you to unpack, and settle in."

He assumed he wouldn't see her again that day, and he cursed the wave of disappointment rolling over him. She wasn't more than a B and B host, an innkeeper. They were sharing a house, but he wasn't entitled to her company. Or to share her bed.

And why did he want to? While he liked people and could throw back a couple of beers in a bar or join the guys for a pick-up game, he was equally content to spend time on his own. He'd done numerous unsupported expeditions in his early years—without a backup of any sort, filming his own trials and tribulations—and was comfortable in his own company.

He should take a walk, explore the town, and grab some food. He needed to give Rheo time to get used to him—he was little more than a stranger.

Rheo sent him a tight smile and whirled on her heel, but her foot caught the edge of the rug. She stumbled and, despite being across the room, he lunged to grab her but missed by a foot. She hit the deck, her arms still at her sides. Her forehead bounced off the rug and she let out an inelegant *whoof.* She lay there on her stomach, her fantastic butt in the air, her head turned to the side. Her mouth opened and closed like a drowning fish.

Fletcher dropped to his haunches, rolled her over onto her back, and immediately clocked the panic in her eyes.

"Keep calm, you've just had the wind knocked out of you. Your breath will come back when you relax."

Her eyes narrowed. Irritation and embarrassment swirled. "Better?"

Rheo nodded. "Getting there."

Fletcher winced at the graze on her forehead. It was a typical carpet burn, and he noticed another on her chin. He touched it gently and frowned at a smear of blood on the tip of his finger. "Why the hell didn't you use your hands to break your fall?" he demanded.

"I have no damn idea. Stupid." Color flooded back into her face, thank God.

"Are you okay? Are you hurt anywhere else?"

"I'm fine, but my pride is in tatters."

Fletch pulled her into a sitting position, and Rheo bent her legs and rested her wrists on her knees. She looked at the ceiling, then at a spot past his shoulder, her feet—anywhere but at him.

"So, it's pretty obvious I have no eye, hand, and body coordination."

He'd noticed. "Do you do this kind of thing often?" he asked, easily keeping his balance while squatting. He inhaled a hit of her, a combination of shower gel and shampoo, and his pants tightened. *Jesus*.

Rheo wrinkled her nose. God, *adorable*.

"Often enough. I once stepped onto a train, stumbled, and caused a row of people to topple like upright dominoes doing a nosedive. I'm a complete klutz."

"You can't be that bad."

"Oh, I can. I once ran into a hotel, desperate to use the restroom. I ran straight into a mirrored wall. The bathroom was across the hallway, and I ran into the reflection."

He scrubbed his hand over his mouth to hide his grin. Okay, he was starting to believe her. "You're also a klutz with a carpet burn on your forehead and chin," he told her, pushing to his feet. He held out his hand. "Next time, put your hands out to break your fall."

"I know that," she shot back. "But the thought came too late. It's like my brain doesn't get those messages. But I can translate—speak and listen to the next sentence in four languages and not so fluently in another two."

She spoke six languages? Holy crap. *Astounding.* Fletcher tightened his grip on her hand and launched her to her feet. But he put too much heft into his pull—accidently on purpose?—and she shot up. This time she remembered to put her hands out and they bounced off his chest.

He gripped her hips—she was as unbalanced as a baby foal—and every nerve in his body went on high alert.

Rheo lowered her hands to hold his wrists, and her thumb drifted over his skin, sneaking under the leather and copper bracelets he wore on his right wrist. Was the skin on her neck as silky as it looked? Was her hair as soft as he imagined? He lifted his hand and ran his knuckle along the cord of her neck and over her jawbone, stopping to wrap a strand of her hair around his finger. Rheo's eyes remained on his chest, so he tipped her chin and her eyes smashed into his.

He'd only seen that shade of blue once before, in Poço Azul, a cave pool in the Bahia region of Brazil. Like that South American pool, her eyes held secrets, as well as confusion and a healthy dose of *Oh, shit—what's happening?* But when his thumb drifted over her full bottom lip, he caught a flash of lust, hot and bright.

He needed her closer, so Fletch placed his hand on her lower back and pulled her to him. Thigh to thigh, chest to chest, a sweet bundle smelling of wildflowers. She tensed, just a little, and he loosened his grip to allow her to push off him, to put some space between them. If that was what she wanted to do.

Rheo's eyes stayed on his, and when she tipped her hips and pushed her stomach into his pipe-hard cock, he couldn't wait a millisecond longer. His mouth covered hers in a move that was far from smooth. As his lips touched hers, his brain signed off, and instinct kicked in.

In all the world, there was only Rheo—she was all that mattered. Her body, soft, feminine, and fragrant, pressed against his, was all he needed.

Fletch tasted strawberry lip balm on her lips as his tongue traced the seam of her mouth, before gently sucking her lower lip between his. She shuddered, gripped and twisted his shirt in her small fist, and sighed, her hot breath hitting his lips. He took the opportunity to slip his tongue into the spice of her mouth. Rheo made a sexy sound in the back of her throat and pushed her hard nipples into his chest, her stomach even more into his throbbing dick.

So good, so freakin' good.

Her fingers streaked through his hair, down his back, but he could only concentrate on her sexy, hot mouth moving under his, demanding more. Demanding *everything*...

A klaxon went off in his head, DANGER written in six-foot-high neon letters.

He was an experienced guy, but her hot response made him want to dive into her, to lose himself.

He was a master of situational awareness—his life depended on it—but Rheo made the world narrow to only her and what they were doing, how she made him feel.

Reckless, impetuous, thoughtless...everything he usually wasn't, and everything he couldn't afford to be. He knew how to compartmentalize, could keep pieces of himself apart, but this woman, with her smooth legs and curves and gorgeous wildflower smell and sexy mouth had his synapses misfiring.

One small hand drifted over his hip, came to rest on his pec directly above his heart. For some bullshit reason, her action was too much, too intense, so he lifted her hand off his body and held it.

Lust, attraction, sex...those were easy to handle. And that was all this was, all it could ever be.

God, he'd met her an hour ago. Why the fuck were these thoughts even running through his head?

Knowing he was on the brink of stripping her and using that big bed, Fletch dialed his passion down, and peppered her jaw with small kisses, before placing his lips on her temple and keeping it there while he waited for blood to reach his brain.

In high-stakes environments, whether it was the Okavongo Swamps of Botswana or pulling a sled across marrow-freezing windswept Antarctica, good decision-making was the difference between life and death. Standing with a sexy woman in his arms wasn't a life-or-death situation, but the rule of making good choices still applied. Sleeping with his new roommate just an hour after meeting her was not, in any scenario, a wise decision.

Not only was she going to be living here and sharing his space for a couple of weeks, but she was also Carrie's cousin, and he didn't want to risk complicating his relationship with a good friend just to get his rocks off.

And, as a few hard expeditions had taught him, when the terrain was too easy and life was too good, that's when he had to pull back and reevaluate. Life had a way of becoming a shit show very quickly.

Pulling away from her took more willpower than it did to pitch his tent in a howling minus-sixty-degree blizzard, but Fletch managed to do it. The sound of their ragged breathing filled the room, and Fletch, who'd hacked his way through impenetrable jungles and survived crazy ice storms, reluctantly admitted he'd never experienced emotional disorientation to this degree.

He'd only just met her, but there was still the lingering worry that if Rheo gave him the smallest hint she wanted to dive back in for more, he'd have her naked so fast her head would spin.

Rheo, thank God, slowly backed away, those extraordinary eyes wider than before. She closed them, shook her head, and ran her fingers across her forehead—was that something she did when she felt off-balance?—and winced when she touched her graze.

She met his eyes and bit her lip. "Well, that was…"

He waited for her to finish her sentence, trying to fill in the blanks. Hot? Unexpected?

"Um…*shit.*"

Did "shit" after a hot kiss mean she was pissed? Could he have read her wrong?

Fuck, he never second-guessed himself, and he'd never, *ever* spent this much time self-analyzing or fixating over what was nothing more than a hot grope and a deep kiss.

Maybe he needed rest and relaxation, and to slow down, more than he thought. It could be that Seb was right.

He could think about that later; right now he needed to make sure Rheo was okay. He hoped she knew he'd never ask for more than she could give. If she had any doubts about him, those needed to be alleviated right damn now. If she wanted to forget about the kiss, they could do that. If she wanted a reset, that was okay too. If she wanted him to leave, he'd be pissed, but he'd pick up his duffel and keys and drive away.

But he'd leave her to explain to her grandmother why his rent wasn't reflecting in her bank account.

He wasn't a complete bastard, but neither was he a saint.

"I—"

Rheo held up her hand, her cheeks red. Why was she blushing? "I'm so sorry if I took our kiss further than you meant to go," she said, her tone measured. "Please forget it happened."

What. The. Crap?

Fletch couldn't make sense of her words, but before he could respond, she walked out of the room.

He stroked his jaw, shook his head, and closed his eyes. *Well, hell.*

It was obvious her mind worked faster than his, and she'd beaten him in the race to see who spoke first. He'd needed more time to boot up his brain, to unfreeze his tongue and rewire his shorted-out circuits.

But unlike him, she'd jumped to conclusions quite quickly. Why was she taking all the responsibility for their out-of-control kiss? It had been a two-way street, both giving, both taking, both *feasting*.

Fletch scrubbed his face with his open palms, linked his fingers behind his neck and tipped his head back to look at the ceiling. *Well, fuck.*

Her effect on him wasn't good.

But their kiss had been absolutely fan-fucking-tastic.

Four

Rheo fast-walked to the stairs, bolted down them, and ran into the kitchen and out the back door. She stumbled onto the path bisecting two beds of sweet-smelling herbs, lavender, rosemary, and lemon verbena. She only knew their names because she'd looked them up.

Stopping at the small paved area halfway down the garden, she placed a hand on one of the four pillars of the wooden gazebo. She'd built the structure a few weeks back, following a YouTube tutorial. Paddy often talked of having one, so Rheo had fought boredom, impatience, and frustration to build her one in the hope it would mollify her grandmother when Rheo fell from grace. She had also bought four concrete pots and planned to plant a gorgeous creeper in each of them—the one with the purple flowers?—so Paddy could sit in the shade on hot summer days.

She was focusing on the gazebo instead of dealing with the problem in front of her. Avoiding the subject was becoming a habit. She'd kissed—no, *kissed* was too tame a word for what they'd done...*inhaled* or *devoured* worked better. She'd devoured Fletcher Wright, and she needed to face her actions and consider the consequences.

Oh *God*. She'd *kissed* him.

Not even an hour after first meeting him, she'd plastered her body against his and tried to sink into him. Sure, he'd returned her kiss, but his reaction was, undoubtably, more instinctive. Anyone would respond when a tongue slid into their mouth and a hand drifted over their hard, spectacular ass.

But he did grip the back of her head to keep her mouth in place, tipped it this way and that, looking for the angle he preferred. He'd pushed his thigh between her legs and his other hand had landed low on her butt, encouraging her to ride his cock. He'd fondled her boob.

Arrgh!

Kissing him whipped her away from this house and her mostly solitary, kinda lonely world. In his arms, with her mouth under his, she'd connected to a previously unknown source of cosmic energy. She hummed with vitality.

While she liked feeling strong and energetic, it shouldn't be a result of kissing some *man*. Standing next to a pretty white wrought-iron chair, she flapped her arms up and down like a demented duck and shuffled from foot to foot. Her source of energy should come from within herself, not from outside sources!

Porca vacca! Holy cows, pigs, and other barnyard animals!

Rheo linked her hands behind her head and stared at her

bare feet, the ring on her middle toe glinting in the sunshine. Right, what should she do? How to handle this? So far today, she'd indulged in some seriously hot eye-on-eye action through her open window, told him he couldn't stay, told him he could, face-planted on his bedroom floor, and then kissed him as if the future of humanity rested on his broad, muscular shoulders.

Could she be more of an ass if she tried? She doubted it.

Rheo buried her head in her hands, feeling the heat of her face. Dropping into the nearest chair, she placed her elbows on her knees and pushed her fingers into her hair. Future Rheo would refer to this period of her life as "the months of excessive humiliation and stupidity."

Through high school and college—she'd endured erratic homeschooling before she went to live with Paddy—she kept her head down and played by the rules. She avoided attention, negative or otherwise. She considered every choice she made and tried to figure out how it would impact her safe, reliable, and secure life.

In the last few months, her reliable boyfriend left her, she created the hot-mic viral video, had her translations corrected—twice—cried in front of her colleagues, and was replaced by another translator when she froze during high-level trade negotiations. She'd crossed the country to hide away in her grandmother's house and was living in it without permission. She was lying to her family, and she'd sucked her grandmother's short-term tenant into her web of secrecy.

And just because she needed to make a bad situation worse, she'd kissed him.

Brilliant work, Whitlock. Truly inspirational.

Rheo wrinkled her nose. She was behaving like her parents—irresponsibly and impetuously—and was ashamed of herself. She'd fallen into a hole and needed to shovel her way out. Or, simply, she needed to get her shit together. No more excuses, no more dumb decisions. No more kissing strangers. She had minimal time until Carrie arrived. She needed to take a hard look at her life and make some rational, unemotional decisions. Her moment—*moments*—of madness were over. It was time to act like the reasonable, thoughtful adult she knew she could be.

A lo hecho, pecho. What's done is done.

She needed to face her mistakes, missteps, and failures. She'd start by telling Fletcher Wright their kiss was a mistake and would not be repeated. She needed to reconfigure her life, whip up another life plan, get her act together. She would not be distracted by a fantastic kisser with big arms, a hard body, and a quirky smile…

But Fletcher Wright had some kissing skills…

Rheo touched her chin and winced. She should clean and disinfect the graze on her chin and forehead, but she wanted to sit here for a little longer. Deep breathing always helped calm her racing mind.

She closed her eyes, tipped her head to the sun, and sucked in another deep breath of the sweet-smelling air. Her heart rate dropped, and her skin stopped prickling. Lust faded away. Unfortunately, her scarlet face would take time to return to normal.

She heard footsteps, and her eyes snapped open. Rheo

admired Fletcher's loose, easy gait as he ambled toward her, one hand wrapped around her flip-flops. Why did he have her shoes? He stopped next to one of the four wooden pillars and their corresponding pots.

Fletcher handed her the beaded flip-flops. "These were lying in a flower bed by the kitchen door, the one with the iceberg roses."

Her eyebrows rose. "How do you know their name?"

There were red roses and yellow, white, and orange…she didn't know any of their names. Rheo took the shoes from his hand with a quick "Thanks."

He shrugged. "My mom was into gardening, roses specifically."

"Where did you grow up?" she asked, sliding her shoes onto her now grubby feet. "You're not American born."

"Scotland, on a smallholding outside Aberdeen."

His statement explained his accent. Rheo lowered her foot to the paving stones and leaned back in the chair, lifting its two front feet off the ground. Right, he was here, and it was time to bite the bullet.

She waved her hand in the direction of the house. "Kissing…" She hesitated, swallowed, and cleared her throat. "It shouldn't have happened."

"You swore, you bolted away, and then, down here, you waved your arms about like a demented chicken. Message received."

Rheo followed the direction of his pointed finger. His bedroom window overlooked this portion of Paddy's extensive garden.

More mortification. *Marvelous.*

"Fletcher, I—"

"Call me Fletch, everyone does," he said, interrupting her.

She nodded her agreement. "My life is complicated, and while I enjoyed kissing you, I'm not in a position to take it any further."

He sent a small, cool smile. "Did I ask you to?"

"Well, no," she admitted. "I just didn't want you thinking—"

"I only met you a short while ago, Rheo, but I already know you think too much." He held up his hand in a silent request for her not to speak.

She narrowed her eyes and waved her hand in a silent gesture for him to continue.

"Firstly, you apologized earlier for kissing me. I was as into it as you, and if I didn't want to kiss you, I wouldn't have."

Okay, that wasn't what she expected. Also, very direct. But she far preferred someone being straightforward than glitter-covered bullshit.

"Secondly, it was only a *kiss*, not a request to take you to bed or anything else."

His *Relax, you're making a big deal out of nothing* was implied, as loud as if he'd screamed it in her ear.

She dropped the legs of her chair to the ground and shot to her feet. She'd heard so many versions of "relax," "stop overthinking," and her favorite, "you're far too sensitive" all her life. The accusation, verbal or not, was a hot-button issue for her and a trigger, instantly reminding her of how different she was from her family and how isolated and lonely she'd felt as a child. How she sometimes—more lately than usual—still felt.

Rheo wanted nothing more than to walk into the house—to go back to New York and her lovely, safe apartment—but before she could, he moved, about to lean his shoulder into a pillar. She threw out her hand, shouting a warning, but his shoulder connected, and the rickety gazebo creaked and swayed. One minute Rheo stood under the roof, the next she was a few steps away, watching the wooden beams tumble to the ground, cracking and splitting as they hit the chairs and concrete slab.

Rheo stared at what was now a huge, messy pile of oversized kindling and wanted to cry. She'd worked so hard on the gazebo, sweating as she sawed, hitting her thumb with the hammer, dropping wooden planks on her shoulder and once on her head. And with one touch of a masculine shoulder, it disintegrated. Okay, she knew it wasn't the most solid structure in the world, but she didn't expect it to fall apart like a pile of pickup sticks.

"Who the hell built that?" Fletch demanded, furious. He held her against him—*nice!*—and she was half off her feet. He'd pushed her out of the way of the tumbling structure and saved her from a serious injury.

She was still processing that reality when Fletch dropped his arm and stepped away from her to kick the plank closest to him. He picked up a concrete pot lying on its side and banged it down on its base. Rheo grimaced. He was properly furious.

"Do you realize how lucky you were? What if it fell when nobody was here with you?" he demanded.

It wasn't a scenario she wanted to think about. Rheo considered asking him whether he could stand up straight for more than five minutes, but decided it wasn't a good time. But why did he always have to lean?

"The posts should've been anchored to the ground with cement." Fletch picked up the end of a beam and inspected a bent nail with disgust. "These should've been bolted in, not hammered together with nails." He glared at her. "Didn't you notice it was rickety?"

Well, yes. She'd had her doubts it would survive when a storm had blown through last week, but it did, so she decided it was fine. To be on the safe side, she'd placed the pots next to each beam to keep them straight and give the pillars extra support.

"I have never come across such shoddy, amateurish workmanship in my life," Fletch railed. "Why do something if you aren't going to do it properly?"

Because she was an amateur? Because she didn't have the first clue about carpentry? Because she was scared of her grandmother, was terrified of disappointing her, and thought a gazebo might make up for her mistakes?

"You need to call the carpenter and demand your money back," Fletch snapped, scowling at the pile of wood.

Now that her adrenaline was subsiding, a bubble of laughter crawled up Rheo's throat. "I can't do that," Rheo told him, her voice shaky.

"Why the hell not?" Fletch demanded, still looking pissed off.

It was time to come clean. About this, anyway. "Because I built it."

★ ★ ★

Rheo walked into the kitchen, shoes back on her feet, and headed for her coffee machine. It was one of the few appliances she'd had shipped from the Brooklyn apartment she'd sublet on a month-to-month lease to the translator who'd stepped into her shoes when she'd left.

The woman had her job and her apartment, the life she'd so carefully created.

Rheo could get it back.

She just needed to get her ass into gear and get back to the organized, rational person she'd been six months ago.

So much easier said than done…

Rheo shoved a cup under the spout of her coffee machine and used the back of her hand to hit the button dispensing magic juice. Coffee-scented steam hit her nose as she carried the cup over to the enormous wooden dining table, one end covered in books and magazines.

Sitting on one of the twelve mismatched chairs around the table, she cradled her cup in her hands and wondered how to act when Fletch returned to the kitchen. She wished she could be sophisticated and oozing with sangfroid, but it wasn't her style. When working, listening, translating, speaking, and listening again, she was a machine, but she'd left her conversational skills in Brooklyn.

Rheo rested her forehead on the wooden table. What lesson was life trying to teach her? And why wasn't she getting it? It would be so much easier if life or God or the universe would just post directions on Instagram or TikTok.

Rheo! Plan the work and work the plan…

You are saving less than fifteen percent of your take-home salary, Rheo! Fix this now!

Turn off your mic when the general assembly isn't in session...

"Mind if I grab a cup?"

Rheo jerked. Fletcher stood in the doorway, filling the space with his bulk. Rheo tipped her head to the side. He really was the most gorgeous specimen.

When Fletcher frowned, Rheo realized she was staring... again. *Please start acting like a rational human being, Whitlock.*

She recalled his question and lifted her cup to point it at the coffee machine. "Help yourself. I'm not sure if there's milk, but the sugar is in the blue canister on the shelf above your head." Right, good job sounding completely normal.

Now carry on in the same vein, Rheo.

"Where are the mugs?"

Of course. A mug would be helpful. "In the cupboard above the coffee machine."

Rheo watched him take a pottery mug from the cupboard, one of her favorites, and place it under the spout. He pushed the start button and turned to face her, leaning his butt against the counter, his feet in well-worn hiking boots, crossed at the ankles. A hot guy was hanging out in her grandmother's kitchen...

Fletch's eyes met hers, and she caught the hesitation on his face. His eyes, no longer shot with lust, were now a matte, impenetrable, seaweed green. Unreadable.

"Can I make a suggestion?"

She lifted her eyebrows and waited. Rheo fully expected a lecture on gazebo construction, everything she did wrong, and why it collapsed. She hoped he'd keep it to under ten minutes.

"For the sake of yourself, your grandmother, and anyone else in your life, please stay far away from power tools, wood, and anything that requires construction. Someone, *you*, could've been seriously injured. Just pay someone next time, okay?" he added, his eyes and expression serious.

That was all he had to say on the subject? She'd take it, and God knew, his comments were more than fair.

"Okay."

His expression reflected his surprise at her lack of argument. She lifted one shoulder to her ear. "I'm just glad it happened now and not later with Paddy. I fully accept I have the DIY skills of a goat."

"But you can translate four languages expertly and can get by in another two. We all have different skills. But yours will never be woodwork." A small smile accompanied his words and he turned his attention back to the coffee machine. "Why did you even attempt to build it in the first place?"

Rheo easily recalled Paddy going on and on about wanting a pretty gazebo in a wild garden after a vacation in England when Rheo was twelve and thought it might go some way in earning her forgiveness for her lack of transparency (i.e., the illegal occupation of her house). She'd looked online, wineglass in hand, bottle close by, and within a few hours had not only ordered the plans for an elegant structure, but also the equipment and materials she needed. The next morning, seeing the dent she'd made in her credit card, she'd felt obligated to attempt to build it herself.

Not her finest moment.

"A bottle of wine and spending too much on my credit card made me overconfident," she informed Fletch.

He didn't pursue the subject, and she was grateful. She didn't want to discuss her complicated relationship with her family and her need for Paddy's approval.

Maybe they could talk about the weather. Or Gilmartin.

"So why don't you want Carrie to know you are here? Where are you supposed to be?"

His questions sliced through the space between them and landed on her skin, hot and unexpected. The words took a moment to sink in. Her coffee machine made its customary rude belch and dripped a few more drops into his cup. Fletch picked up the cup, took a sip, and joined her at the table, stretching out his long legs.

She cleared her throat. How should she answer his question? She couldn't, obviously, tell him she'd been at odds with her family for as long as she could recall or that she was the drab cuckoo in a nest of brightly colored macaws. Unlike her, he clearly didn't wrestle with the world, and didn't need to fight for his place in it. He seemed happy in his skin. Would anything faze him? She couldn't imagine him feeling insecure or being able to understand the uncertainty of always standing on the outside looking in.

She eventually answered him. "It's complicated."

"Aren't families always complicated?" he replied before lifting his cup. "Great coffee, by the way."

It was a monthly delivery from a specialist coffee shop

in Brooklyn. "Kenyan. It's a blend I stumbled across a few years ago."

"I like it," he stated, looking past her counters and through the back door onto her garden. "The garden is magnificent. Your work?"

Ah, he'd noticed he'd hit a nerve and was attempting to make her feel comfortable. Sweet of him. And it was working. "God, *no*. I once tried to grow herbs in pots on my foot-wide balcony in Brooklyn, but I never remembered to water them. And I don't cook."

Amusement jumped into his eyes. "Right. You live in Brooklyn?" he asked.

"Yeah, up until four months ago. I'm hoping to go back soon, if I can work my way through the madness of the last few months."

He tapped a blunt finger on the rim of his mug and pounced on her statement. "What happened?"

Rheo pulled a face. Why had she said that? She wasn't in the habit of blabbing about her work screwups. Wasn't in the habit of confiding in strangers, period. But Fletch didn't feel like a stranger. Not now and not when they'd kissed. Indescribably delicious, he'd sent blood flowing to parts of her she'd long forgotten. Despite never having met him before, she recognized him. Being in his arms, her mouth under his, felt right. Normal.

Wild! She didn't believe in instant connections, nor did she believe in love at first sight. *Coup de foudre* was French romanticism. Magnetism and desire she understood, as they were biological impulses, but wandering off into Romance Land was silly.

And she wasn't silly. She was practical and pragmatic, a planner. Anything *but* silly.

Needing to change the subject, Rheo tossed out a question, hoping his answer would assuage her curiosity. "So, what work do you do for Carrie, Fletcher?"

He sent her a low, slow smile, the mental equivalent of being dipped into a vat of rich, warm, silky dark chocolate. She loved dark chocolate…

"Why do you think I work for Carrie?"

Um…she was sure there was a reason. *Oh, right.* "Earlier you said you'd worked as a sound guy and a cameraman."

"I have, but not for Carrie," he told her. "I make my own documentaries."

Great. Fletch being someone who flitted around the world, exploring, documenting his travels, made complete sense. She'd felt the wildness in him earlier. Another nomad.

That he and Carrie were friends didn't surprise her. Carrie avoided nine-to-five men and held a great deal of disdain for anyone who wore a suit and worked set hours—Rheo especially. Corporate men bored Carrie. She always said they were insanely tedious, and she'd rather hook up with a store mannequin. Since Rheo enjoyed set hours, loved coming home to the same apartment, and knew what her next week, month, and year looked like, she took exception to her cousin's statements.

Carrie didn't give a rat's ass whether she was offended or not.

"What's your show called?" Rheo asked, mostly to be polite. She wasn't into watching anyone wandering around old cities, eating street food, and taking in the tourist attractions. Occasionally doing a bungee jump or zipping from tree to tree.

"My most recent one is *A Year in the Jungle. A Year in Ice and Snow* will be released in a few months."

She'd never heard of them and told him so. Fletcher shrugged and didn't seem annoyed that she'd never seen his work. Unlike Carrie, who thought everyone should watch her being brilliant.

"They have a bit of a following with people who like adventure. I've done some hardcore expeditions."

She wrinkled her nose. According to Carrie, most adventure/travel content creators weren't half as tough as they claimed to be. "So, do you only pretend to sleep in a tent and sneak off to sleep in a big double bed in the nearest five-star hotel?"

Fletcher took another sip of his coffee and smiled. "There weren't any five-star hotels where I went." He stood and nodded to her cup. "Would you like a refill?"

Grateful he'd asked, she nudged her cup in his direction. Fletcher turned away and Rheo looked at his broad back and spectacular ass. It took a lot of time and effort to get as fit and as strong as he was. Unlike her. If she was ever found dead in a gym or on a jogging trail, the most likely explanation was that she'd been murdered elsewhere and her body dumped.

Fletch turned back to face her, his expression imperturbable. "So, I guess we should discuss us living together for the next week or so."

Rheo thanked him for her coffee. "Why *is* Carrie coming here?" Carrie put everything on social media, including a rough schedule of where she'd be and what she'd be doing, frequently reminding her followers that she was a free spirit and liable to change her mind at any second. Since she was heading for Gilmartin sometime soon, that meant caving in Vietnam must be on hold. "I thought she had a full schedule until the end of the year."

"She said she needs a break and wants to recharge. All the stuff we like to do for fun—hiking, trail bike riding, and free climbing—is easily accessible here. As I mentioned, we also want to kayak the Little White Salmon."

"Sounds fun," she lied.

He hit her with a *don't bullshit me* stare. "Why don't you want Carrie to know you're here, and how do you intend to explain your presence when she gets here?"

Because we don't speak much. Because I didn't tell her or my parents I had a meltdown. Because we have different worldviews.

Rheo didn't have any idea of how she was going to explain her presence in the house. Yet.

Rheo answered his last question and ignored the rest. "I'll just tell her I made an impulsive trip to check on the place." She shrugged, knowing he wouldn't believe her breezy reply. Fletch looked laidback and easygoing, but his eyes moved constantly, taking in data and processing it.

"Why do I suspect you don't do anything on impulse and your trips are planned months in advance?"

Ugh, he made her sound *too* straitlaced. "I can be impul-sive," she retorted. "I've made last-minute trips. I can be spontaneous."

She hoped he didn't ask her for dates and times, because she knew she couldn't back up her heated statement.

"When?" he countered, moving her mug so she didn't knock it over with her waving hands.

His eyebrows lifted and she caught the challenge in his gaze. She wasn't someone who played games—she preferred to walk away from confrontation, especially when she was out of her depth. But something about this big, bold man made her want to go toe to toe with him.

"When were you last impulsive, Rheo?" he pushed.

"When I kissed you twenty minutes ago!"

Rheo bit her bottom lip, shocked she'd let those words fly. She normally enjoyed complete command over what left her mouth; it was the way she earned her living. She always chose the right words, the *appropriate* words. Well, mostly. With one or two major exceptions.

Fletcher lifted his mug and looked at her over the rim, his eyes boring into hers. She held her breath, waiting for his reply. She stood on the edge of a golden, electrified cliff, teetering, about to fall into a miles-deep chasm. He made her *feel*, and Rheo didn't like it.

Emotions could be very annoying.

"We did kiss," Fletcher replied in a nothing-out-of-the-ordinary-here voice. "I definitely didn't anticipate liking it so much."

Rheo sucked in her breath and planted her ass on the chair

and her feet on the floor. He looked as tense as she felt. They both understood that if they moved, their clothes would start flying and Paddy's table would see some action.

Knowing what the rest of her family were capable of, Rheo was pretty sure it wouldn't be the first time.

Fletcher ran his hands over his face.

"You being Carrie's cousin complicates things," Fletcher quietly stated after a long silence. "I think it would be better if we ignore our chemistry so there's no... awkwardness when she arrives."

Because, sure, the world would stop if Carrie experienced some awkwardness. And of course there would be awkwardness; there always was when she and Carrie occupied the same room. They were oil and water.

But it didn't matter. She had no intention of sleeping with Fletch. Sorting her life out was a priority; having sex wasn't. She was crunched for time and couldn't waste her mental energy on a man.

"I agree," Rheo said.

And if she had any *I'd like to share the sheets with you* thoughts while she worked out what to do or where to go, she'd just ignore them.

Fletch nodded, walked over to the fridge, and pulled open the door. He looked back at her, a little horrified. "Rheo, something is growing in your fridge."

Rheo looked at the container in his hand, and through the clear plastic, she saw bubbles of black-and-green mold. *Eeeww.* She'd bought the cheese from Abi, never ate it, and forgot to take it out. She existed on pizza, takeout, and microwave meals, and because she didn't drink milk, she rarely went into the fridge.

"I'm going to have to buy some food," he said, sounding perturbed.

"Don't let me stop you," she told him. "There's a great deli on Main Street that's owned by my friend Abi, and the store around the corner stocks pretty much everything."

"What do you live on?" Fletch demanded, dumping the cheese into the trash can and turning to the sink to wash his hands. "Fresh air?"

Rheo gestured to a door behind her. "In the walk-in pantry, there's a chest freezer stocked with meals Abi makes. I'm a genius at peeling, pricking, and pinging. And I'm great at ordering takeout."

Fletcher closed his eyes and shook his head. "To thank you for letting me stay, I'll cook and you'll eat."

No problem there, given that she possessed the domestic skills of a houseplant. "Deal. Are you a good cook?" she asked, curious.

Fletcher sent her a *get real* look. "Since you only have moldy cheese and a couple of cans of soda in your fridge, I can only be better than you."

Excellent point.

Five

In her childhood bedroom, Rheo pulled back the covers on the old-fashioned brass bed and slid under the cool sheets. She inspected the fan above her head. Like everything else, it needed a good dusting. Paddy normally hired a team to spring-clean the house in April. Did her normally on-the-ball grandmother forget to do that this year, or was it another sign Paddy was losing interest in the Pink House?

Normally, she'd ask, but since Paddy didn't know she was here…*blah blah blah.*

Honestly, Rheo was surprised her presence in Gilmartin had remained a secret for so long. Sure, she'd been an infrequent visitor since she graduated college, but she'd expected someone to recognize her by now. Then again, according to Abi, the neighborhood had changed over the past five years. There was a huge demand for holiday houses in Gilmartin, and many older residents chose to cash in and sell. The residents Paddy knew well were either dead or had moved on, so Paddy couldn't be that influential or well-known anymore.

The town was so different now, and Rheo was grateful. The last thing she needed was a nosy neighbor sending Paddy a message, updating her on Rheo's every move. She could only hope the gazebo crashing didn't raise anyone's suspicions. Thank God the yards were big, and the houses were spaced far apart. She might've gotten away with it—at least she prayed she had.

Rheo recalled Fletch's disgust over her handiwork. Okay, so carpentry wasn't her strong suit. Yes, she vaguely remembered something about placing the pillars in concrete, but it sounded like a lot of work, so she skipped that step. Her lazy mistake could've resulted in someone getting seriously hurt. The next time she attempted a project, she'd follow all the steps. Do it properly.

Or, a far better idea, get a professional, as Fletch so rudely suggested.

Fletcher Wright…another adventurer. Why couldn't her unexpected roommate be someone who worked in accounting or banking? Someone with a steady income, a healthy 401(k), a homeowner, and someone who saved ten percent of his income since he'd started working?

She had enough nomads in her life, thanks bunches. He was a complication and a distraction she did not need.

Rheo yawned. What a day! It was the most eventful one she'd experienced in months. She needed sleep but doubted she'd get it. Her brain was in machine-gun mode.

Her phone beeped with an incoming message. Abi. *Shit!*

She'd forgotten to contact her. Her messages hit her screen, one after the other.

Well? Who is he?

What happened to pizza?

Why don't you tell me *ANYTHING*?

Ah, because, in between Fletch's arrival, face-planting, kissing him, and the gazebo collapsing, updating her friend had dropped down her priority list. Rheo decided to mess with her a little.

He's spending the night!

Excellent!

Damn, she'd forgotten Abi was unshockable.

Do you need me to do an emergency condom run?

No, Abs, he's sleeping in the guest bedroom.

Disappointing. ☹

Rheo saw the dots on the screen and waited.

Tell me everything!

Rheo briefly explained who Fletch was and the day's events, including her fall but leaving out the kiss. She also omitted the gazebo crashing.

So, have you googled him yet?

Well, no, but that was a damn good idea. Rheo told Abi she'd call her in the morning and ended their chat.

Rheo plugged his name into a search engine, thinking she should know more about the man she was sharing a house with to justify her actions. She was a woman alone; it was smart. It had nothing—*liar, liar*—to do with her curiosity.

His website was the first result in a long list, but a podcast titled "Q&A with Fletcher Wright" caught her interest.

She tapped the Play button, and the nasal voice of the interviewer blared from her phone's speakers. She hit the pause button and grabbed her AirPods, thinking she didn't want to risk Fletch knowing she was cyberstalking him. Silly. His room was on the other side of the house and there were many walls between them.

"Adventurers, here's a taste of our podcast interview with one of our favorite modern-day explorers, Fletcher Wright.

"Regular listeners, millions of you, will have heard me interview Fletch Wright before because I've followed his career for years—you're thirty-five now, right? I encourage you to listen to our previous podcasts on exploring the Dasht-e Lut, the Kalahari and Taklamakan Deserts. He's climbed Everest and numerous other peaks, and has hacked his way through parts of the Amazon, the Darién Gap, the Congo, and Papua jungles."

So, he was a proper, grown-up explorer. And he was more, well, *famous* than he'd implied. Interesting.

"Thrilling stuff. I can't wait to dive in, we have so much to talk about! But, as an icebreaker, we're going to start, as we usually do, with the questions sent in by you, our listeners. So, here goes… What is your biggest pet peeve?"

Fletcher's deep voice poured into Rheo's ears, and she couldn't help squirming a little in response. *"The sound of Styrofoam squeaking. It makes my ears bleed. It also takes about five hundred years to break down in a landfill."*

Rheo placed her head on her pillow, happy to listen.

"What occupation, other than your own, would you like to try?"

"I like making stuff, using my hands. So, yeah, I guess I'd love a huge workshop where I could build shit, but only when I've run out of places to see. The world is big and that might take a while."

Irritation spiked, hot and unwelcome. Yeah, his statement sounded familiar. Carrie and her parents always talked about their next trip and the one after that. They spent more time thinking about where they were headed next than enjoying where they were. Fletch seemed to be the same.

It made her sad, and Rheo didn't understand why. He wasn't boyfriend material, and her imagination wasn't vivid enough to see him as a long-term partner. Why was she even going there? A man in her life wasn't a priority! Sorting her life out was. She'd had a suitable boyfriend, and *he'd* wanted more than *she* could give…

"If you could live anywhere in the world, where would it be? Have you bought a place yet, or are you still living out of your van?"

Oh, God, he owned a van. Seriously? *Ugh.*

"I upgraded my van to a tiny house, which I parked at the end of a friend's property in Portland. It can still be moved, so I haven't gone over to the dark side."

The interviewer laughed, and Rheo narrowed her eyes. There was nothing wrong with wanting the stability of staying in the same place. Before her meltdown, it had given her a sense of security she'd never known as a child, and she wished these van-life-loving, chasing-freedom types—her parents, Carrie, and Fletch—would stop judging people who liked conformity.

Rheo lifted her phone to kill the podcast, but the interviewer's next question captured her attention. *"If you could have coffee with any modern-day or historical explorer, who would you choose? Edmund Hillary? Charles Darwin? Ed Stafford?"*

"Ed and I are more likely to have a beer than coffee. The others sound interesting, but I would choose the botanist Jeanne Baret. Back in the 1760s, she was the first woman to circumnavigate the world. She disguised herself as a man and was employed as a valet to the expedition's naturalist. I think we can all agree she had a big set of balls."

Except for the circumnavigating the world on a ship thing, Jeanne Baret sounded like her type of girl: independent and smart.

"Is that your ideal woman? Someone with a big set of balls? Your name's been linked with Carrie Whitlock, the travel influencer and an adventurer."

Rheo paused the podcast and checked the publication date. It was recorded a few weeks back, so this wasn't outdated information.

"Carrie and I are friends. And, yes, I like friends, and lovers, who can keep up with me. I enjoy people who challenge me, physically and mentally."

Well, that was that. Their kisses were hot enough to spark a wildfire, but sexual attraction was all they had in common. He was a nomad, lived in a van—*sorry, tiny house*, but still on wheels—and hopped from destination to destination. Rheo didn't have a hope in hell of keeping up with him on the mildest of outdoor hikes. She was a sloth; he was a mountain goat.

Mentally, she could match him. She had a postgrad degree and an active mind. She read widely—okay, she didn't know about Jeanne Baret, but she was pretty sure Fletch didn't know the Italian alphabet only had twenty-one letters. She enjoyed interesting and stimulating conversations, arguing principles and debating ideas.

Rheo checked the time left on the podcast. Just a few minutes to go. She'd listen to the end.

"If you could go back and give your eighteen-year-old self one piece of advice, what would it be?"

"Honestly, I would tell people to go fuck themselves far more often than I did."

"Wow. Don't hold back, Fletch," she whispered aloud.

"What are you bad at?"

She knew the answer to this question. He wasn't tactful and he didn't pull his punches. *"Being patient and diplomatic. I don't do hints, subtle or obvious. If you want me to know something, just spit it out."*

Nailed it.

"What's the one thing you'd rush into a fire to save?"

"Two books. King Solomon's Mines *by H. Rider Haggard and* Into the Wild *by Jon Krakauer. After reading them as a kid, I became obsessed with traveling."*

She'd read neither and vowed she would. But only because they were classics. There was a gap in her literary education; it had nothing to do with Fletch and what he read as a kid.

"What's your biggest fear?"

The interviewer was getting into deeper waters now, and Rheo doubted Fletch would answer. She didn't know him well, but she suspected Fletch didn't volunteer information, personal or otherwise.

"Fletch, your biggest fear?"

Fletch's sigh was audible and his voice lowered, a fraction sadder when he spoke again. *"I'd hate it if I had to stay in one place for the rest of my life. Being confined."*

Rheo turned over Fletch's words, surprised by his sincerity. Why did he feel so strongly about being confined? She wanted to know.

"Then I suggest you avoid jail…hahaha." The bad joke broke the tension. *"Right. How big is your inner circle?"*

"Not big."

His answer surprised Rheo. With his looks and charisma, she expected him to have lots of friends. She imagined him to be like Carrie, who commanded attention and had hordes of people trailing in her wake.

"What's the one thing you'd never change about yourself?"

Fletch didn't hesitate. *"My self-reliance."*

She respected his answer. She made her own decisions

and owned her mistakes. True, she'd made more than usual lately, but they were hers to make, hers to own. And she'd learn from them. Maybe not today or tomorrow, but at some point in the future.

"And that's a perfect segue into talking about your latest adventures. For those living under a rock, Fletch has spent the last twelve months exploring the North Pole, the South Pole, and for kicks, summited Mount Everest without oxygen."

Why would he *do* that? Why would *anyone* do that? The whole it's-there-so-I-must-conquer-it argument made no sense to her. Why put your life in danger, risking frostbite and hypothermia and rockfalls to climb a mountain? The mountain didn't give a rat's ass whether you got to its highest point or not.

"How did you find it, Fletcher?"

"Cold."

Rheo grinned at his pithy answer and enjoyed his dry sense of humor. The interviewer thanked Fletch for his time and started thanking his sponsors, so she exited the podcast and placed her phone on the bedside table. As she removed her earbuds, her screen lit up with an incoming call.

Paddy. Of course it was, because life wasn't done with kicking her ass today. *Shitshitshit.* Was she calling about the gazebo? Because someone saw Rheo talking to Fletch?

Rheo considered ignoring her call, but Paddy would just call back. Then she would send her a series of messages and a flurry of emails. It was easier to answer. Rheo greeted Paddy, amazed at the clarity of their call.

"It sounds like you are around the corner," Rheo said.

"I want to see your face, I'm desperate to video call you," Paddy complained. "I can't understand why we always have such bad connections."

Ah, that might be because Rheo always dropped the call if she was somewhere Paddy might recognize. Like her kitchen. Or garden. This bedroom.

"It's a mystery," Rheo breezily replied.

Paddy told Rheo about her trip, and Rheo listened, enjoying her grandmother's sharp wit and perceptive observations. She wanted to be just like Paddy when she grew up. Strong, opinionated, independent, and financially free. Paddy had taken the money her ex gave her in the divorce, bought a few houses, and flipped them. Then she bought some apartment blocks and managed those for most of her life. At seventy, she employed a manager and moved into fundraising for charities, using her forceful personality to open wallets. At eighty, she decided she needed to see the world and opted to visit Australia first. Rheo was pretty sure Paddy had the country whipped into shape already. Rheo adored her, but her grandmother scared her.

Just a little.

After Rheo batted away Paddy's questions about her life and job—"all good, nothing to tell"—Paddy changed the subject.

"How are your parents?"

"Fine, I guess. I haven't heard otherwise." Rheo sighed.

For the past eighteen months, Rheo's dad and Paddy had waged an ongoing war about whether or not Ed had demanded to see his mother's will. Paddy said he did, that Ed wanted to know what he could expect to inherit from her, and that her money was his retirement plan.

Ed insisted that he'd only asked Paddy whether she *had* a will, but Paddy vociferously disagreed. Knowing her dad's irresponsibility, and his lackadaisical approach to money and the future, Rheo believed Paddy. But Ed could be extraordinarily stubborn on occasion, and he wasn't backing down. As a result, mother and son hadn't spoken for over a year. Messages and news passed through Rheo during their bi-weekly calls and monthly emails.

Rheo, tell your father…

Rheo, tell your grandmother…

"Where are they at the moment?" Paddy asked with a less than normal vigor.

Rheo frowned, needing a moment to think. "Somewhere in Western Canada. I haven't spoken to them lately."

"I presume you've been very busy with the UN General Assembly being in session."

"Mmm-hmm." There were omissions and there were outright lies, and Rheo tried to avoid the latter whenever she could, so she switched subjects. "Where are you? Still on the Gold Coast?"

"I'm staying at a superb inn in the Barossa Valley, quaffing truly excellent wine and eating superb food."

The poor woman was having, obviously, a *miserable* time. Rheo's heart bled for her.

"I'm thinking about staying longer, another month or two at least."

That would put Paddy's return at the end of August or September. Not that it mattered—Rheo would be out of here soon. "Okay. Are you returning to Portland, or will you swing past the Pink House?" she asked, trying to sound casual.

"I'm not sure. Did you hear that I've rented the Pink House? To a friend of Carrie's, but I'm sure he's her lover."

Not a lover! Rheo wanted to protest, but kept her lips welded together.

"I need to think about what to do with the Pink House, Rheo," Paddy continued. "It's empty more often than not and needs serious maintenance. It's been a lovely indulgence, but the costs are rising."

"But you love this house," Rheo spluttered. "You can't sell it!"

"Who said anything about selling it?" Paddy pounced on her words.

Rheo cursed. She'd made it through a long and stressful day, and wasn't up to sparring with her grandmother tonight. To be fair, she seldom was. "Sorry, I assumed that's what you meant."

"Something is going on with you, Rheo Jane," Paddy murmured after an intense ten seconds of silence.

Rheo mashed her lips together. If she jumped in with a denial, she'd never hear the end of it. Paddy would dig and dig, and Rheo would cave.

She couldn't. Currently, she wasn't strong enough to face Paddy's criticism or deal with her disappointment. Paddy never let her down—she loved her, supported her, and didn't try to change her. When Rheo had a plan in place, a way forward, when she'd fixed her mess, she'd confess all and take her grandmother's criticism on the chin. For now, she'd keep her silence for as long as possible.

"I must go," Paddy declared. But she still had one more bullet to fire. "How's that young man of yours... Colin?"

"Callum?" Rheo corrected her, guilt dancing under her skin. "He's fine." She hadn't heard anything to the contrary. She wasn't lying...*technically*.

"Stable, steady, but not exciting," Paddy commented, getting a dig in. "He sounds as impressive as a white crayon."

Her grandmother was smart but possessed the ability to strip wallpaper with her tongue. The fact that she was also right was intensely annoying.

"Be nice, Paddy."

"I speak my mind because it hurts to bite my tongue."

Rheo tipped her head back to stare at the ceiling. While her grandmother understood her need for stability and approved of her independence—financial and otherwise—she'd made it clear that Rheo's predictability didn't need to extend to men. Paddy believed Rheo should have excitement in the bedroom and assumed Callum wasn't the man for the job.

She wasn't wrong. Fletch's kiss packed more punch than the lukewarm orgasms Callum had managed to pull from her. But predictability was safe. She knew what to expect.

Rheo didn't like roller coaster rides. And Fletch was the biggest, baddest ride out there.

Six

Chúpamela!

Rheo jabbed her finger on the pause button on her video and cursed again. She flung a ballpoint pen against the wall, wincing when it left a black streak on the cream paint.

Over the past ten days, since Fletch's arrival, she'd spent a lot of time planning her return to New York City. First on her list of priorities was to find out how rusty her translation skills were. Like most things, simultaneous translation required practice, and she hadn't spoken Spanish, or any other language aside from English, for many months.

Biting the bullet, she'd downloaded training manuals for translators and spent a few hours every day moving up through the various levels. Once she got into the swing of it, the first two levels were easy, but today's sessions—each two hours long—were much harder. She'd fallen way behind, and her Spanish word choices were consistently inaccurate. Thinking she might have a block with Spanish—the language of her biggest failure—she'd switched to French, and the results had been equally disastrous. There had been nothing simultaneous about her efforts.

Alone in Paddy's office, with only a machine judging her, she fumbled her words. If she couldn't get it right here, with no one applying pressure, how could she return to her job? Nicole expected her to come back with the same or better skills, and Rheo was way off. Way, way off.

Dear God, this was an ongoing nightmare.

Rheo heard a knock and hastily minimized the program before telling Fletch to come in. He strolled through the door, a little sweaty, a lot sexy, carrying two water bottles. Rheo swallowed, trying to keep her thoughts out of her eyes and off her face. Her nipples were out of control. It wasn't fair he was so damn sexy, that every atom in her body reacted to him on a cellular level.

Whenever he entered a room, fireworks exploded under her skin, the moisture in her mouth disappeared and the ache between her legs intensified. She wasn't particularly sexual, but Fletcher Wright, adventurer and the last man in the world she should be attracted to, just *did* it for her.

Rheo took the bottle of water he offered and leaned back in her chair, watching as he walked over to the window and pressed his shoulder into the wall. Fletch never stood when he could lean…

His pale gray sleeveless vest dipped low enough to show most of his chest. Unsurprisingly, he wore running shorts and a pair of well-used sneakers. On the days he wasn't leaving early for a hike, a kayaking session, or rock climbing, he always went for a run. Watching Fletcher jog down the street, heading for one of the many trails in the hills surrounding Gilmartin, had quickly become the best way to start her day.

"How far do you run?" she asked him, happy to be distracted from her interpreting shortcomings.

"Normally fifteen, but my doctor won't let me run more than six miles at the moment."

Fifteen miles? Why would anyone want to run for so long unless end-of-world zombies were chasing you, threatening to suck out your brains?

"Why only six?" she asked.

He swallowed half his water before answering. "He says my body has taken a pounding and he wants me to rest," Fletch replied, sounding grumpy.

"And has it?"

He lifted one bare shoulder in a dismissive shrug. "It's his opinion."

"An opinion built on experience and many years of study," Rheo said, her tone dry. Fletch hated being told what to do, that was obvious. "Did you get hurt on one of your expeditions?"

"I put myself in hard-to-survive situations. There's always a chance of getting hurt," he replied. He didn't answer her question, which was an answer in itself.

"You only ever walk to your friend's house or the deli," Fletch said, turning his sharp eyes on her. "Why don't you go for longer walks? Why don't you run?"

Oh God, he wasn't going to lecture her, was he? There was nothing worse than an evangelical fitness fanatic. "I hide from exercise. I'm in the fitness protection program."

Fletch didn't smile, and Rheo threw up her hands. "C'mon, that was funny!"

"You'd enjoy hiking if you did it a bit more, got a bit fitter."

Rheo leaned back in her chair and rested her hands on her not-so-flat stomach. "You're confusing me with my cousin," she told him. "She's the adventurer in the family... Actually, that's not true. Everyone in my family is obsessed with the great outdoors except me."

The Pink House's basement contained snowshoes and skis, ropes and carabiners, canoes and paddles. The Whitlocks could open a store with all the equipment they'd purchased and collected over the years. Rheo made a point of avoiding the basement. Whenever she went down there, she remembered she was the gray dove in a flock of brightly colored flamingos.

"Why?"

Looking into his lovely eyes, Rheo wanted to tell him the truth. But how could she explain how out of sync she felt without sounding whiny? Would he understand that she preferred books to boulders, languages to ledges? She couldn't bear a lecture on how much she was missing, what she could learn from expanding her horizons, or how she would come to love it if she just gave it a chance. She'd heard it all before—over and over and over.

"I have no natural stamina," she informed him. It was the truth.

Fletch, as she expected him to, frowned. "What do you mean?"

"One of the reasons I'm not into trail running or hiking is because I tire easily," Rheo explained. On the few occasions she'd tried to join in on a family hike, she'd struggled to keep up, and her family found her slow pace annoying. "I can move quickly when I have to, and I can do stop-and-start exercises, but I've never managed to run more than two miles without feeling like I am going to die. Honestly, during a zombie apocalypse, I'd rather let them eat me than run for my life. I'll sacrifice myself so the rest of you can get away."

His smile caused her breath to leave her body in a single *whoosh*. "Early in my career, I hired a cameraman who was the same. A fantastic guy, very creative, but despite training hard, he couldn't build up enough stamina for long days and miles of slogging. Letting him go was hard, but necessary. I had to put his safety, and the safety of the team, first."

Fletch nodded at her laptop. "You looked like you wanted to stab someone when I walked into the room. What's the problem?"

She wrinkled her nose and wondered how much to tell him. "One of the reasons I'm in Gilmartin is because I've hit a snag at work…"

"Define a snag," he demanded after her words trailed away.

She rubbed the back of her neck. "Currently, I'm not translating at a UN standard level," she admitted.

His thick eyebrows rose. "I would say that's less of a snag and more of a problem."

Precisely. "Yeah. It's one of the reasons I was forced to take a six-month sabbatical," Rheo admitted. Would he ask what the other reasons were? She hoped not—she wasn't ready to give him that much information yet. She lifted the lid of her laptop and gestured to the screen. "These are training videos. We use them to brush up on our skills when we've been away from the job for a while. Maternity leave or when we move from one language section to another."

He sat on the edge of the desk, facing her. "Language section?"

"The UN Translation Service has language sections, like Spanish or Italian or Arabic. I worked in the Spanish section, but because I'm fluent in French, Italian, and German, I could work in those sections too. If I got transferred to another section, I'd use these programs to make sure my skills are up to standard."

"And you don't think they are?" Fletch softly asked, placing his big hand on her shoulder.

She shook her head and chewed the inside of her lip. "No," she admitted. When she looked at him, she saw his curiosity and attempted to explain.

"I can still speak the languages—" they'd taken a little holiday, had some time out, but hadn't deserted her forever "—but I'm second-guessing myself. I don't know if I'm understanding the context correctly or choosing the right words to get the meaning across."

Fletch's shorts rode up his muscled thighs, and she wanted to brush her fingers through the soft hair on his legs, wanted the anchor of her hand on his skin.

She shook her head. She couldn't expect anyone else to make her feel in control. She relied on herself, and it was dangerous to seek assurances from other people. Other people weren't reliable.

Fletch looked from her to the screen and back again. "So, you have the words, but it's the meaning you're struggling with?"

"Mmm-hmm."

He shrugged, lifting his hands. "Sometimes, when I can't find a route through an obstacle, across a glacier, or through a section of jungle, I tend to get tunnel vision and I forget to look for other options. When I step back and take a few minutes to relax, my jumbled mind clears, and the way forward becomes easier."

She considered his words. He'd nailed it. She was doing that. By trying so hard to get it right, she was second-guessing her word choices and making it ten times harder than it needed to be. When she was in the zone, time flew, and the words tripped effortlessly off her tongue.

But how could she relax when there was so much on the line? Her career—and the life she'd spent so much time constructing—all rested on her going back to work and doing what she did best.

Right now, she was far from her best.

Fletch touched her hand with the tip of his index finger. "One day I hope you'll tell me why you're on a sabbatical, Rheo, and why you're hiding out at your grandmother's house. I'd like to know why no one knows where you are or what you're going through."

She wanted to tell him, and that shocked her. Explanations danced through her mind, desperate to be verbalized. She ached to talk to him and explain the decisions she'd made.

Why? Why Fletch? She rarely spoke to anyone, even Paddy. She never described her inner landscape and seldom shared her thoughts. Words and languages were her thing, she earned her living from them, but she couldn't verbalize what she felt inside.

Yet she could easily imagine telling Fletch more than she'd

told anyone. Stupid, because they weren't even friends! They shared a house, but they'd spent little time together over the past ten days. Carrie was arriving soon, and Rheo was leaving.

Though only God knew where she was going. Her apartment was currently occupied and Rheo, the queen of planning, didn't have a plan B. Plan A was also proving hard to nail down.

Rheo sent Fletch a tight smile and pushed her chair back. They had two days left together, so what was the point of sharing anything when she was halfway out the door? "It'll all work out. I'm not worried."

Biggest.

Lie.

Ever.

She was terrified to the soles of her feet and was rapidly running out of options. Carrie's arrival meant Rheo had one of two choices: coming clean or moving out. She wasn't ready to explain, to eat humble pie—admitting to her family how she failed was worse than the failure itself—but she didn't have anywhere else to go.

She could stay on Abi's sofa for a few nights, but that wasn't a long-term solution. Returning to Brooklyn wasn't an option either—she'd have to rent another place for a month and her expenses would eat into her savings. Wherever she went, she'd have to pay to rent a place. And get a temporary job to cover her accommodation costs.

But where? How?

That was her problem, not Fletch's. Rheo tossed her water bottle in the trash basket. She was on her own and running out of options. And Fletch was a complication, a distraction.

She gestured to her screen. "I've got to get back to work."

Rheo waited for Fletch to close the door behind him before resting her forearms and head on the desk. Yes, she was frustrated and overwhelmed, but she wasn't finished. That would only happen if she gave up and quit. She'd checked out for four months, but she was back in the game. Sort of.

But, crap, it was harder than she remembered.

Two days later, Fletch stood in the kitchen, idly making scrambled eggs and splitting his attention between his food and the view. After almost two weeks in the Pink House, he expected to feel scratchy and antsy, ready to move on, but he'd yet to feel restless or hemmed in. Yesterday, he'd spent the day hiking, and today he planned on hanging out in the hammock strung between the two huge western hemlock trees at the bottom of the garden. He'd found a book on David Livingstone's exploration of the Zambezi in the library, and he was eager to dive into the world of the nineteenth-century explorer.

He'd been for a run and Fletch was, strangely, happy to do nothing. The only irritation was his low-hum attraction to Rheo, an itch that wouldn't go away. He'd expected the attraction to have faded by now but, nope, it was still there, bigger and brighter than before. And he spent far too much time imagining them naked, together, in bed.

His phone pinged and he glanced down at the message on his screen.

Shit, Fletch, I'm sorry. Am still in Hanoi, I've picked up food poisoning. Obvs, I'm not going to make my flight and I need to get better quick because I have a meeting with a producer who wants to talk to me about a travel program for Netflix. I will probably not get there for another few weeks. Sorry to break your heart, but stay in the Pink House for as long as you want! You understand, right?

Fletch pushed his annoyance away. The stomach bug couldn't be helped, and he wouldn't pass up an excellent business opportunity to fly home for a holiday either. He'd delayed some of his Gilmartin adventures to share them with Carrie, and she wouldn't be here for ages. But he wasn't going to wait around for her. He would schedule the Little White Salmon run for just before he left, one day of hard exercise couldn't hurt him, surely? He'd also find a climbing party keen for him to join them, and sign up for some hikes. Compared to his normal exercise regime, running, light climbing, and hiking were well within Seb's orders. The residents of Gilmartin knew he was in town, and having some clout, adventure guides would fall over him to make his adventuring wishes come true. There were upsides to being semi-famous.

He liked this town, enjoyed the vibe, and felt at home in Paddy's house in a way he'd never experienced before. Houses, hotel rooms, even his tiny house in Portland, reminded him of being confined as a teenager, and any room he spent too much time in soon started feeling like a prison.

Having spent a year confined to a bed, Fletch valued his freedom above all else and reveled in his pick-up-and-go lifestyle. His quest for freedom went deeper than physical movement. It was, in a weird way, symbolic of his recovery and triumph over CFS. And, yes, ridiculous or not, he was scared that staying in one place for too long might somehow push him back into confinement and illness. Being fit and constantly on the move was his way of reassuring himself he was healthy and free. He wasn't wasting his second chance to live life fully.

He shook off his thoughts and pulled in a deep breath. The walls of *this* house had yet to start closing in on him, so he was good for another week or two, maybe even three.

He didn't need Carrie to enjoy the area, but how would Carrie's news impact Rheo? She was leaving in a day or two, and he'd found himself dreading her departure. He had no idea why, especially since they hadn't spent much time together.

He'd avoided her because of their hair-trigger attraction. He always scanned the horizon for trouble, and after that kiss they'd shared on his first day, he knew that if he and Rheo ended up in bed, and Carrie came back to Gilmartin, he'd have to juggle his time between the woman he was sleeping with and his adventure-loving friend.

Spending his nights with Rheo and his days with her cousin seemed sketchy, so he'd kept his distance. It hadn't been easy.

And Rheo avoided him because… Who the hell knew?

But if Carrie wasn't due back to Gilmartin for a few weeks, then there was no reason for Rheo to leave right away. Would she leave anyway? He had no idea. His stomach knotted.

Rheo affected his inner compass, made him feel like he was a few degrees off, less confident in his direction, and unsettled. He was a man who rarely second-guessed himself, but Rheo made him feel off-balance and curious. Normally, he'd be running for the hills, so he wasn't sure why he was eager to keep that feeling that way, but he was.

Fletch tipped his eggs onto his toast. The kitchen door banged open. Rheo stood in the doorway and stepped out of her dirty flip-flops. Over the past week, he'd heard lots of cursing coming from her study—he presumed she still wasn't as fluent as she needed to be. Some words he recognized, some he didn't, since she flipped between languages.

When she had enough of whatever she was doing in there, she worked off her frustration by weeding her grandmother's garden. He wasn't much of a gardener, but he could tell a plant from a weed. Rheo, unfortunately, could not. And he wasn't brave enough to tell her.

Rheo lifted her hair and twisted it into a messy bun on top of her head, securing it with a band she kept around her wrist.

She had a streak of dirt on her nose and grubby hands. She declined his offer to share his eggs.

Fletch sat at the kitchen table as Rheo washed her hands. Her tight vest showed the straps of her hot pink bra, and her ragged denim shorts traced the gentle curve of her spectacular ass. The table hid how much he appreciated the view.

His phone rang, flashing an unfamiliar number, but he recognized the Gilmartin area code. Only the adventure supplying brothers had his cell number.

"Mick? Or Sam?" he asked, mouthing *sorry* to Rheo.

"Mick. Sam's run out for coffee," the older of the two brothers replied.

"What's up?" Fletch asked, placing his ankle on his opposite knee.

"We have two hardcore trail runners coming in at the end of the week, and they've booked a run with us. We wondered if you wanted to join."

"Hardcore" meant distance and difficult terrain and long hours. The type of exercise Seb had forbidden him to do. Fletch should say no right now and not waste Mick's time.

The devil on his shoulder danced. "How long?"

Mick replied quickly. "Forty miles."

"Elevation?"

"Six thousand feet."

Hard but usually very doable. "And what time do your clients want to clock?"

"Between six and six and a half hours. Sam regularly runs those sorts of times."

That was fast, and it would be a challenge for him to keep up. Fletch liked challenges. Then he remembered Seb's directive to take it easy and silently cursed. He could ignore what Seb said and do the run. He felt fine, and Seb would never know.

Except that one of Louie's nephews would tell Louie and Louie might mention it to Seb and his friend would wipe the floor with him.

Besides, if he couldn't do something openly and honestly, then it wasn't worth doing. *Dammit.*

"Next time," he reluctantly told Mick and quickly ended the conversation before he changed his mind and disobeyed his doctor's orders.

"What's up with you?" Rheo asked. "You look like a bear with a sore paw."

"Have you ever seen a bear with a sore paw?" Fletch demanded. God, he sounded like a cranky toddler.

"What's put you in a foul mood?" Rheo asked, drying her hands.

Being unable to do what I want… His health was an off-limits subject and so was the urge to kiss her again, so he told her Carrie'd had a change of plans.

"She won't be here for nearly a month," Fletch told her, then forked eggs into his mouth.

There was no hiding the relief in her eyes, the way her body sagged as tension seeped out of her. Carrie's change of plans suited her.

"What's her excuse this time?" Rheo asked, keeping her tone light. "Is there a mountain she needs to climb, a dive she has to take? Is there a man she has to see, a temple she has to explore?"

He heard a hint of resigned irritation in her words. What had caused the issues between the cousins? Carrie was fun and outgoing, and she didn't owe him her time. If she wanted to change her plans, she could. Like him, she didn't bind herself to anyone. She could move at a moment's notice, and they both liked it that way. Yeah, he was disappointed not to have her company in Gilmartin, but he couldn't be pissed off about it. There wasn't one set of rules for Carrie and another for him.

"Actually, she's got a stomach bug and won't make her flight," Fletch told Rheo, his voice cool.

Rheo's smile seemed a little sarcastic. "I'm sorry to hear that. But I bet you a hundred dollars something else cropped up. There's a fish she's trying to hook, a catch she's trying to land."

He couldn't deny it. "She's got a meeting with a TV network producer," he admitted.

Rheo snapped her fingers and pointed at him. "And there it is," she said. "I can't tell you how many times Carrie has changed her plans at the last minute."

Rheo dropped into a chair opposite him and leaned back on its two legs. She bit the inside of her lip, her expression a little anxious. He knew she wanted to ask whether she could stay, whether he'd give her another few weeks at the house.

She wasn't ready to leave, and for some reason, he couldn't figure out why he wasn't ready to let her go. But he couldn't help wondering how she'd ask him... Would she dance around the subject? Would she ask without frills and fuss? Or would she chicken out and leave?

Rheo put her chair down, her elbow on the table, resting her chin on her clenched fist. This woman had so many layers, and he wanted to peel them off one by one.

A ripple of terror chased up his spine. He enjoyed peeling off clothes, but going skin-deep was as far as he ventured. Relationships required sacrifices he wasn't ready to make, and he had no interest in working out what made a woman tick. Rheo, damn her, tugged uncomfortable feelings to the surface.

A part of him hoped she left the Pink House and Gilmartin, and took her big eyes, her tempting body, and her vulnerability somewhere else. The rest of him wanted to take her right here on her grandmother's kitchen table.

She lifted her head and her eyes slammed into his. "Carrie's delay doesn't change anything, Fletcher," she told him. "I said I would go, and that is what I should do."

Should. She said "should," and that one word was a cracked door, a sliver of light.

"You don't have to if you don't want to," he said, his voice deeper than normal. He pushed an agitated hand through his hair. If she wouldn't ask, he'd tell her. "If you want to stay, that's fine."

Then he added, "And I won't tell Carrie you're here."

"Thank you, I appreciate that. I'd like to stay."

She reached for his phone and spun it around. She liked to fiddle with things when agitated. He wasn't a master of zen either. He was on a mental surfboard, feeling a mammoth wave rising underneath him. It would either be a great ride, or he'd wipe out spectacularly.

He frowned at the flash of frustration skipping across her face. "Am I missing something here?" he demanded.

Rheo sent him a smile as old as time and full of promise. A smile that made him lose his words. His shorts tightened across his lap. Rheo crossed one tanned thigh over the other and he nearly swallowed his tongue.

"Look, I know that I'm not wildly good at flirting," she said, "but I've noticed you looking at me. I've certainly done my fair share of looking at you, and you've caught me once or twice. I think you're attracted to me—"

Think? His eyes followed her every movement, and it took all his willpower not to make a move every hour of every day. He leaned forward and waited until she met his eyes. When she did, he kept his tone low, but definite. "I'm *very* attracted to you, Rheo."

She nodded, closed her eyes, and scrunched up her nose. "I'm tired of pretending I don't want you, Fletch. I'm tired of lying in bed, wishing you were with me, wishing your hands were streaking over my skin."

Holy crap. Okay, then. He was about to make a move—hadn't she given him a green light?—but Rheo motioned him to sit.

"Hold your horses, cowboy," she murmured.

His horses were way out of control, and judging by the glint of amusement in her eyes, she liked his eagerness.

"Spit it out, Rheo," he muttered. He looked at his hand, shocked to find his fingers trembling. This woman wanted him and it made him *tremble.*

Pull yourself together, Wright! Who are *you?*

"I'd like to stay in Gilmartin for a little while longer, Fletcher," Rheo said in her precise way. "But I also want to sleep with you on a let's-have-fun-while-we-can basis."

He was on board. So, so on board.

"As long as you know there's nothing more to my offer than some fun between the sheets. I'm not looking for anything more."

Fletch frowned. That was his line, and she'd delivered it with aplomb. Unfortunately, her words didn't ring true. Not because Rheo didn't believe what she was saying—he could tell she meant every word—but because she deserved more. She *should* be in a relationship. Rheo should have someone to love and support her. Not him but someone…

You're overthinking this, Wright. She'd offered and was waiting for his answer.

He wanted Rheo, Rheo wanted him…

Rheo looked anxious, like he was about to reject her… Jesus, how wrong could she be?

He stood and held out his hand. She slid her smaller hand into his. "Are you sure?" he asked.

"Very."

Fletch nodded, dropped her hand, bent his knees, and in one smooth movement, lifted her and tossed her over his shoulder in a fireman's lift.

He heard the *whoomph* of her surprise and her small fist smacking his back. He walked out of the kitchen and jogged up the stairs.

"Fletcher! What the hell are you doing?"

He kicked open the door to his bedroom, pulled her down his body, and dumped her onto his bed. She pushed her hair out of her face, and he was relieved to see laughter in her eyes.

He shrugged and grinned. "I'm taking you to bed, and I intend to keep you here for the next few hours. Is that okay with you?"

Her smile smacked him in the solar plexus. "Yes, very okay. But your delivery needs work."

His delivery, now and later, would be just fine.

Seven

Fletch pushed Rheo's hair off her forehead, unable to wrench his eyes off her. Rheo was why his blood was hot, why his heart flip-flopped around his chest. Blue eyes and thick hair, mystery and marvel, secrets and shadows. And right now, she was the air he needed to breathe, the thump of his heart, the sigh of his soul.

Fletch touched her delicate jawline with his fingers, marveling at her scented smooth skin. He rested a thumb in the middle of her bottom lip, waiting to taste her because when he did, he'd devour her.

Lust, shocking and bright, powered through him, and he swayed, momentarily dizzy. He didn't want to start because one kiss would bring him closer to an end.

He didn't want this to end.

Yes, he wanted her, and he'd thought about this moment more often than was healthy. He wanted her when she made him smile—she had an extensive vocabulary of curses in six languages, and he was pretty sure he heard a Russian phrase the other day when she was arguing with her computer. When she sat on the step leading up to the kitchen door every morning, soaking in the sun as she slowly sipped an enormous mug of coffee.

She didn't need to fill every moment with inane conversation, and at night, he loved stepping into the bathroom after her, savoring the steamy scents he only caught hints of during the day.

Fletch shook his head, irritated by his flight of fancy. He was a practical guy. As Rheo said, this was about sex. One night, some mutual pleasure. It had nothing to do with magic or moonbeams or fantasies.

He didn't believe in forever.

But he still didn't want to start…

Rheo pressed her lips against his, cool and smooth. She looped her arms around his neck, and her fantastic breasts, high and round, pushed into his pecs. Her scent, full of floral notes, filled his nose, and her hair fell over his hands as they rested on her back. He wouldn't, couldn't let go.

Relinquishing his self-control would be like riding a rocket, surfing a storm wave. Wildfire scary.

"Fletch."

It was just his name, murmured against his mouth, but it was also a key to a lock. Nobody before had said his name the way she did, coated with need and a hint of *What was happening here?*

"*C'est dingue!*"

There it was; the foreign phrase he'd been expecting.

French? He had no idea what it meant, but it sounded sexy, and since her hands were streaking up his back, he presumed it was something complimentary.

Gripping the back of her head with his hand, he put his lips to hers, needing to explore the shape of her mouth, the contours of her lips. His hand skimmed up the back of her thigh, sliding under the denim to skim the curve of the butt he eyed any chance he got. He pressed the pad of his thumb to the middle of her bottom lip—the lip that got a little pouty when she didn't get her way—and when her mouth opened to release a pleasure-filled gasp, he slipped inside, his tongue curling around hers. Pleasure rose and fell, built and built, as he changed angles...

She tasted of spice and sweetness, of sin and sex. And with every swipe of his tongue, he hardened, his cock straining against his zipper. He ached to have her. But not in a race-to-have-an-orgasm way; he wanted to see her skin flush with pleasure, to watch her blue eyes cloud with lust. He wanted to know whether they'd lighten or deepen when she came.

Kissing Rheo was like riding a fast-moving river, negotiating one thrilling rapid after another. A swoop of his stomach, a kick of his heart, a fall, lost in the white water of her kiss, finding air. Wild, wet, thrilling.

Rheo's hands, elegant and clever, skated over his rib cage and tugged his shirt to find his bare skin. Her nails scraped his flat nipple, causing it to pebble. Rheo ripped his button-down shirt apart, and buttons flew, the material fraying. He didn't give a shit. He liked that she was as desperate for him as he was for her. Dropping his hands from her body, he allowed her to push the shirt off his shoulders, and didn't care when it fell to the floor in a tangled heap.

Fletch kissed his way down her throat, across her collarbone, and pulled her vest and bra strap down her tanned arm. He sucked the top of her breast, rubbed his chin over the lacy cup of her bra, grazing it with his teeth. When she whimpered, he sucked her nipple, fabric and all, into his mouth. Rheo shuddered, and his name was both a curse and a prayer on her lips.

"Miss your mouth," Rheo muttered.

Fletch took her lips and fed her long, slow kisses. Kisses with no beginning and no end. Rheo's hands skimmed across his body, eager to discover the next bit of skin, the next bump in his spine. She pushed her palm down the back of his pants held up by a thin leather belt, growling when she couldn't cup his ass.

Fletch lifted his head to smile at her. "If you want my clothes off, honey, just ask," he teased.

Rheo astounded him by reaching for the button on his jeans. "I'm more of a take-what-I-want type of girl."

There was a hint of bravado in her voice, some hesitancy in her eyes. Maybe she was projecting confidence she wasn't feeling.

"If that's okay with you?"

"Very."

His zipper came apart and her hot hand held him in a tight grip. Pleasure shot into his balls, up his spine.

She moved her hand, rolling it up and down, and his eyes rolled back in his head.

"Oh, hell yeah, so fucking okay." He was impressed he managed those few words.

Rheo's thumb brushed the tip of his cock and delicious shudders skittered over his skin.

"I think we need to get a little more naked," she murmured.

Fletch watched as she stripped for him. Her movements were economical, efficient, but still fucking sexy. The moisture in his mouth disappeared as he took in her curves and her amazing skin. He hooked his thumbs under the thin cord of her sunshine yellow panties and pulled them down her thighs. Now deliciously naked, he pulled her to stand between his thighs, his hand sliding from collarbone to knee. So soft, so silky. Placing his mouth on her sternum, he inhaled her. His head swam.

She was heaven—soft, feminine, exquisite.

But she could also be hell if he wasn't careful.

Fletch hooked his hands around the back of Rheo's thighs and moved his mouth to her pussy. When he licked once, she gave a muted scream, and he did it again, twisting his tongue around her clit. He looked up as Rheo rocked her hips, demanding more. He licked and sucked, pushed his tongue and his fingers up her slick, wet channel.

Years ago, a lover told him she thought oral sex was more intimate than normal sex, that it required more trust. He never understood her reasoning, but he thought she might be onto something. Rheo was completely submissive to him, to his lips, fingers, and tongue.

She writhed and rocked, her soft panting music to his ears. He worked his finger and his mouth in and over her folds, sucked her clit, and relished her incoherent moaning. Inside her, he tapped his fingers against her inner wall, sucked her hard, and felt her come, waves of pleasure hitting his fingers, his tongue, and his lips.

Fletch pulled away from her, enjoying her side-swiped expression and shaking body. He'd done that. He'd made her come. Hard. His arm around the back of her legs held her upright and her body flushed pink with pleasure.

When their eyes collided, he clocked her *What the hell just happened?* expression and gently laid her on the bed. He leaned over her and waved his hand in front of her face.

"Rheo? Are you okay?" he gently asked, sliding his thumb over her bottom lip. His cock was so hard, he was desperate to be inside her, but he needed to check where she was at. "Rheo, talk to me."

Her unfocused eyes met his. "That was so good. So, so, amazingly good. Do it again."

He grinned. "Glad you enjoyed it. And in a minute."

She waved at his cock. "I didn't do much…sorry."

"You didn't need to. I loved every second of making you come."

Rheo tapped his hip with the tips of her fingers. "Okay then. Thanks. Going to take a nap, then a shower."

For just a moment, he thought she was serious. But then he noticed the quick lift of her lips, the naughty glint in her eyes before she closed them. Right, two could play that game.

He lowered his head, smiled against her mouth, and dragged his finger through her wet folds, flicking her clit. She lifted her hips, groaned, and sighed.

When her eyes opened, when they met his, she wasn't teasing anymore. "More."

"More?" he repeated, lifting an eyebrow, his finger on the inside of her thigh.

"I need you to fuck me, Fletch."

"I need to fuck you more."

He moved so the head of his cock probed her folds and her heat.

Wrapping his hand around his dick, he stroked the tip over her clit, and her eyes widened. She was close, silently begging to come again.

Fletch fumbled for a condom in his bedside drawer, and with Rheo between his knees, pulled the latex from its cover. Rheo's hand, soft and silky, joined his and he gritted his teeth to keep from exploding in her hot palm.

With the condom on, Fletch slid his hands under her butt, scooted back, and swiped his tongue against her clit. She shuddered, so he did it again. Then, in a swift movement, he replaced his mouth with his cock. He fed her a hot open-mouth kiss—nothing felt better than being inside Rheo.

Warmth. Wet, hot woman.

He held still, wanting to enjoy the moment, but Rheo jerked up, slamming his balls against her. He gritted his teeth—he was so damn close, and then she milked him, her channel gripping him tight, her body trembling under his. Unable to hold back, he slammed into her, then again, and as his balls contracted, as he exploded, she came again, a warm, wet flood against his tip.

Then, because this was Rheo, he came, just a little, again.

Fletch buried his face in her neck, and somewhere, in the minuscule part of his brain still functioning, he quietly admitted sex so profound, so earth-shatteringly good had to have its roots in something deeper than attraction.

The thought scared the shit out of him.

Convinced Fletch was asleep, Rheo slipped out of his bed and walked over to the L-shaped window seat in the corner of the room built to take advantage of the magnificent view. Pulling on one of Fletch's T-shirts—the neck fell halfway down her left shoulder and the hem hit her knees—she sat on the window seat and leaned back.

A full moon turned the garden ghostly in its silver light— and turned the trees the deep green of Fletch's eyes when he was turned on or laughing. Slinky gray skimmed the forest, the surface of the lake, and the slopes of the mountain. It was sometime after midnight, and she was physically exhausted. Rolling around in bed with Fletch had expended more of her energy than she'd expected, but her mind was in a spin cycle. Sleep was a long way off.

She'd had sex with Fletch...fantastic, hot, *sexy* sex. And, somehow, strangely, deeper than she'd expected it to be.

She'd thought they'd connect on a purely physical basis, Tab A would slip in Slot B, but the past few hours had proven it to be more complicated than that. Fletcher was a tender but fierce lover, someone who refused to allow her to skate along on the surface. He'd demanded her full involvement in their pleasure, mental and physical, and he'd claimed, and received, every bit of her focus.

She'd never experienced such intense sex before. No man had turned her inside out the way Fletcher did. She covered her face, blushing at the thought of him between her legs, knowing every inch of the most private parts of her. He'd run his fingers down her butt, flirted with her butthole, skated through her grooves and channels. Good at his job as he was, there wasn't a part of her left unexplored.

She felt sexually wrung out, but relaxed. Both on a high and chilled to the max.

Her disparate feelings, the intensity of what happened between them, how at ease he made her feel about her body— they all added layers of complication she didn't want or need.

She'd loved it, loved being with him, loved every minute of how he made her feel. For the first time, she felt as if the combined power of all her female ancestors flowed through her veins. She'd made him grunt, moan, and shout with satisfaction. With her hands and lips, teeth and tongue, she'd brought him to his sexual knees, and she hadn't believed that was possible.

With Fletch, she felt more like a woman than ever before. More her. More Rheo.

You haven't had sex for a while. You've never *had exceptional sex, and you're overreacting, making more of it than you should.*

Overreacting and second-guessing herself were her superpowers.

Rheo gently banged her head against the wall behind her and scowled at the silver-gray moon.

She was terrified that sleeping with Fletch was the last entry on her list named Bad Ideas. They were the definition of opposites attracting. All they could ever be was a fire that burned hot and quick and died out as fast.

She'd told herself he was trouble, but she'd opted to stay at the Pink House even after she learned Fletcher was renting it. She should've taken his arrival as a sign to confess her secrets to her family. But instead of biting the bullet, she'd stuck around, hoping for a miracle.

Miracles don't spontaneously happen, dummkopf!

Anyway, she didn't deserve a miracle—all her problems were self-inflicted. Unused to navigating big bumps in her normally smooth life, from the day of the hot-mic incident, she'd overreacted and made things worse. Instead of throwing up her hands and admitting she'd screwed up, she'd indulged in mental self-flagellation and punished herself by making more mistakes, each worse than the last.

And she couldn't forget the part pride played. In her family, she was the one who didn't make mistakes, or at least not big ones. She was the stable, serious individual who could be relied on to make the correct decision at the correct time in the correct way. Because her life was normally smooth sailing, and she'd looked down on her parents and cousin for their fly-by-night lifestyle. As a result, karma was now snacking on her ass.

Moonbeams hit her legs and feet and, despite having just shared the most intimate act two people could, loneliness swamped her. Paddy was her sounding board, her source of clear and concise advice, but because she'd shut Paddy out of her life, she couldn't cry on her shoulder.

And, God, what was she going to do about her job? Her

online translating sessions were going a little better—bad was now *meh*—but she wasn't up to the standard the UN required. If she couldn't do her job, what would she do? How would she live, keep her apartment and her lifestyle?

And, a bigger question, who would she be?

She'd spent most of her life designing adult Rheo, and she couldn't redraw the map now. How would she explain to Paddy that she'd fucked up on a cosmic scale? Paddy wasn't easily impressed, and Rheo craved her approval. She'd had so little encouragement and understanding from her parents as a child that she valued Paddy's validation, hard as it was to earn. She probably put too much emphasis on it, but needing Paddy's approval was part of her DNA.

She couldn't keep focusing on the past. Rheo needed to turn her attention to the future. How could she improve her skills and, more importantly, get her confidence back? She hadn't lost her ability to communicate; she was simply terrified to get anything wrong. Unfortunately, confidence wasn't a switch you could flip, a tap easily opened.

She used to be good at her job, but her battered self-worth made her agonize over word choices, and she put too much emphasis on getting it right.

Something hard nudged her shoulder. She looked up to see Fletch, dressed only in low-riding sweatpants, holding wineglasses. He'd tapped her shoulder with a bottle of red wine. She hadn't heard him leaving the bed or the room.

"Do you want a glass?" he asked, sitting opposite her.

Rheo nodded. "I'm sorry, I didn't mean to wake you," she told him as he poured red wine into a huge goblet.

"Your thoughts are unbelievably loud, Rheo." Fletcher passed her a glass. After tipping wine into his glass, he placed the bottle on the floor. He leaned back against the opposite wall, bending his long legs. He gestured to the moonlight-soaked vista beyond the window.

"That's one hell of a view," he quietly stated. "I forgot it was a full moon. If I'd remembered, I would've gone for a hike. There's nothing quite like walking in a forest in the moonlight."

She darted a glance at him. "I never pegged you for a romantic, Wright."

"I'm not, and I always prefer to do any night walks alone. They're good for thinking. You should try it sometime. You might find some answers out there."

Not even a burning desire to sort her life out would convince her to go into the woods at night. Even in the moonlight.

"Or you can talk to me," Fletch suggested. "Because, God knows, you need to talk to someone. You remind me of a corked bottle about to blow."

"Charming," Rheo muttered, but she couldn't argue the point.

Rheo took a few sips of her wine and rested the foot of the glass on her thigh. She might as well tell him some of it. She couldn't go into all the details—too embarrassing—but she could tell him enough for him to get a general idea.

"I messed up at work, then I messed up again. And again. It... *I* spiraled out of control. I was offered—no, it was strongly *suggested* I take a sabbatical. I sublet my Brooklyn apartment and came here, where nobody would look for me."

Fletch didn't speak for a long time. "So, why doesn't anyone in your family know you are here?"

He was asking her to wade into deeper waters. "Because I'm not the type who messes up at work, who has meltdowns. I'm the sensible Whitlock, the stable Whitlock, the one who doesn't find herself in hard-to-navigate situations."

"As your cousin does," Fletch murmured.

"I've never been detained by border police, deported from countries, been kidnapped in Colombia, nor have I spent time in a Thai jail."

Fletch's smile was full of affection. "Carrie never managed to get a handle on her paperwork. I don't know why not, because she's not a dumb girl," he explained. "She was deported from *one* country for not having the correct work permits, and she was briefly detained by a couple of kids in Bogotá pretending to be a bigger deal than they were. She spent the day with them teaching them how to play poker. Her stint in a Bangkok jail was a case of mistaken identity. She plays up her bad-girl antics on social media because they get more clicks and a bigger reaction, Rheo."

Oh. "Then why didn't she tell *me* the truth?"

"Did you ask her what happened? And would you believe her if she told you the truth? Carrie once told me you like believing the worst about her, and she didn't want to disappoint you."

Oh God, there was enough truth in his words for them to sting.

She *did* like believing that Carrie was a screwup and that

she, in having a stable job and a career, was the better of the two cousins. She had her shit together; Carrie didn't.

God! She was so arrogant and patronizing!

Rheo stared at her feet, knowing she couldn't examine her feelings toward her cousin right now. She had no wish to take herself apart and examine her ugly interior, because God knew what else she would find. More things she didn't like about herself?

Luckily, Fletch changed the subject. "What do you think your biggest problem is, Rheo? Right now?"

That wasn't a hard question to answer. "Work. My career."

"Okay. Why?"

"After a couple of stressful weeks, I was translating for a very important trade deal when I lost my words," she explained.

He swung his legs off the seat and rested his forearms on his knees, his glass of wine dangling from his fingers. "You lost your train of thought?"

She wished. "No. I lost my words. I stood there and I couldn't speak, not in Spanish or Italian or French or German."

"Ah…*shit.*"

"I asked to be excused and they sent in another translator. My boss referred me to a psychologist, who diagnosed severe burnout and work-related stress. They recommended a four- to six-month break."

"So where are your words?" he asked, his eyes on her face, looking into her. "Have they come back?"

Rheo rocked her hand from side to side. "Sort of. I mean, I can speak the languages again, but I'm not understanding as quickly as I need to. I'm second-guessing myself, and I have no confidence in what I'm doing. I'm not nearly ready to go back to work, and if that doesn't change soon, I won't have a job at all."

Fletch had furrows in his hair from her fingers, and his bare chest glinted with silver moonbeams. "What's stopping you from getting back to the level you were at?" he softly demanded.

"I'm scared I'll make a fool of myself. I'm scared to fail. I'm scared I won't be as good as I was."

"That's a lot of scared, Rheo," Fletch said. He poured more wine into their glasses before sitting with his back to the view. "Fear can be a great motivator, but you have to keep control of it. A little can go a long way, and too much can be destructive."

"You sound like you know what you're talking about," Rheo said.

His smile seemed strained. "I do. Fear is the one thing I can talk about with great authority. I've lived with it and danced with it. We're old acquaintances."

Rheo moved from her seat to sit cross-legged next to him, her knee resting on his thigh. "Will you tell me, Fletch?"

Maybe if she looked at the emotion through his eyes, she would see it differently, learn how to work with it or cage it.

She placed her hand on his thigh and bit her bottom lip. "It's fine if you don't want to talk. You don't have to, obviously. I just thought it might help me make sense of my situation."

Fletch took a huge swallow of wine and bent to place his

glass on the floor next to his feet. "Since you have little interest in outdoor activities and less, I presume, in explorers, I need to ask whether you heard about the earthquake and avalanche in Nepal in 2015?"

She didn't live under a rock, she told him. "An avalanche annihilated the base camp at Everest, right?"

"Parts of it," Fletch agreed. "I was in base camp at the time, preparing to summit Everest."

Holy shit. Rheo stared at him, her eyes wide. She recalled the news footage of the flattened tents, the ice-covered faces of the survivors, and the shock and desperation in their eyes. Given half a chance, her parents and Carrie could've been there—all three had expressed a burning desire to hike into base camp, soak up the atmosphere, and walk a little of the path that took climbers to the top of the world.

"I'm not going to describe the noise, loud and terrifying, or the screams. I briefly thought my life was over, and I'd die at the bottom of the mountain I'd come to conquer. We caught the outer edges of the avalanche, and one of the tents belonging to my team was obliterated."

She needed to ask. "Did you lose anyone?"

He shook his head. "No, but some of my team were injured. A broken leg, a concussion, cuts, and stitches. When the worst of it was over, those of us who could walk and function helped out. We wrapped up the dead, carried the living to medical tents, and coordinated food and shelter. There was a lot to do."

"I can imagine," Rheo murmured. Such a lie. She couldn't begin to.

"We were stuck there for some time, and when there was nothing more we could do, we hiked out. It took us a couple of weeks to walk back to Kathmandu, and we passed through decimated villages. Kathmandu was unrecognizable. There's something about a natural disaster that shakes you to your core."

Rheo rested her forehead against the muscled ball of his shoulder.

"On the plane flying out, I didn't think I could go back. And I didn't, until last year."

"Why did you go back?"

He took some time to answer. "I made a few promises to myself as a teenager. One of them was to climb Everest, preferably without supplemental oxygen. After the avalanche, I couldn't face going back, but I knew I would betray my younger self if I didn't."

Rheo watched his face in the dim light, as the moon had disappeared behind the one cloud in the sky. His expression was remote, and she knew talking about his Nepalese experience wasn't easy. And God, she loved him for doing it, for trying to explain his experiences with fear so she could deal with hers.

"We raised more money—it costs a fucking fortune to climb the peak—and we went back last year. My Nepalese Sherpa kept asking me if I was in the right frame of mind and whether this was something I wanted to do. He was a wise old guy and knew I wasn't fully committed mentally."

"Were you scared?" Rheo asked.

"No. I was fucking *terrified*," Fletch admitted, his eyes

clashing with hers. "I didn't want to be there. I was on constant high alert for any rumblings suggesting an avalanche was coming down the peak. I was a basket case. In hindsight, I think I was suffering from a little PTSD."

"I would be surprised if you weren't," Rheo commented.

"I hid it well," Fletch continued. "Only my Sherpa knew anything was wrong. One day, on the Khumbu Icefall, I fell apart. The icefall is, believe it or not, one of the most hellish and dangerous places on the mountain. Many people have lost their lives there. You have to cross these incredibly deep crevasses, and while you are clipped into a fixed rope, it's not for the fainthearted. I started to cross a ladder, got halfway across, and froze. I simply couldn't move." He smiled softly. "I suppose it would be similar to what happened to you when your words disappeared."

"Yeah, much the same," Rheo responded, before fiercely adding, "except my life wasn't in danger!"

His smile broadened just a fraction. "I was roped up. But on that ladder, I had to decide whether my Everest dream started or ended there, whether I'd let fear win and go home. So I started talking to it, treating it like it was someone on the trip with me. I told Fear he could hang around, but he had to shut the fuck up. He was only allowed to talk when he had something important to say. He wasn't allowed to keep muttering in my ear, pointing out every perceivable danger. He was there with my permission, and I was tired of his shit."

Rheo cocked her head, listening carefully.

"Sounds weird, right?" Fletch asked her.

She shook her head. "Did it work?" she asked. Stupid question; she knew he'd stood at the top of the world.

"Yeah. I reached the summit four weeks later."

"It took you four weeks to walk up one mountain?" she asked, horrified. "God, why would anyone want to do that?"

He laughed. "No, we go up the mountain to higher camps, then come down again, partly to stock the camps, mostly to acclimatize. We spent weeks on the mountain before I made the final push," Fletch explained.

"And Fear, did he shut up?"

"Mostly," Fletch replied, his tone low. "He'd start at three in the morning when the wind howled and the mountain creaked. He grumbled a lot, but I never allowed his voice to become loud enough to drown out my desire, my need, to conquer that fucking peak."

He hadn't loved it. He'd climbed Everest because he had to, because he'd regret it if he didn't.

"Would you go back?" she asked, but suspected she already knew the answer.

"To Base Camp?" He shook his head. "No, I don't think I will. Not for a long time anyway. There are other mountains to climb, other peaks to be scaled."

Rheo placed her cheek against his shoulder and sighed. "My losing-my-words-trouble seems so small compared to yours," she said, linking her fingers in his.

Fletch turned and placed his hand on the side of her face, lifting her chin so their eyes met and held. "You can't compare fears or pain or lives, Rheo. Just because I had a panic attack on Everest and you had one in a meeting room of the

UN building doesn't make mine better than yours. They both affected us in different ways. One wasn't more impactful than the other. If anything, I think yours had more impact. It forced you into a different life and you ended up here."

"Because I ran away," she muttered.

"Or maybe you retreated to gather your strength and re-group."

Fletch was being kind, nicer than she expected him to be.

Rheo did feel her battle with fear was more of a gentle hike than a scramble up a dangerous-as-hell mountain. But if he could face his fears on an icefall in some far-off country, why couldn't she face hers here, in the Pink House? If he could make his fingers move and his legs work to cross crevasses on rickety ladders, why couldn't she find a little confidence to believe in herself and what she did?

She wanted to, she did, she just didn't know how. But she had to. Somehow.

Fletch kissed her temple before dropping his head to kiss her mouth. "Come back to bed, sweetheart. Let me love the worry out of your mind."

"Can you replace it with a solid dose of courage, and a backbone while you're at it?" Rheo asked as she followed him back to bed.

He smiled, his thumb tracing the outline of her lower lip then placing a hand on her chest, just above her heart. "It's in there somewhere, Rheo. You've misplaced it, not lost it."

As Fletch pulled his T-shirt off her body and stepped out of his sweatpants, she desperately hoped he was right.

Eight

After another spectacular night without sleep—why waste time sleeping when he could have sex with Rheo?—Fletch yawned as he walked into the office of his favorite guide outfit in Gilmartin. Although smaller and less slick than the bigger, more established operations around town, Mick and Sam radiated authenticity and had Louie's same can-do attitude. They worked hard, were hungry for business, and gave their clients personalized attention.

Fletch, who'd interacted with many outfits over the years, hoped they'd make a success of their fledgling business and, as they grew, hoped they'd keep the personal touch.

He stepped inside their open-plan office and immediately sensed the tension in the room. He looked from one worried face to another. "What's the problem, guys?" he asked.

"How can we help you today, Fletch?" Sam asked, clearly trying to be professional.

Fletch appreciated the effort. "I want to hire you guys

for a solo climb sometime early next week. I'd like to try Devil's Crack."

Mick walked to the counter where their computer sat and opened their booking program. He gave Fletch a date that suited him, then told him a bit about the route and what he could expect.

After a minute of Mick's prepared speech, Fletch cut him off. "You can tell me later. Now, what's the problem?"

Mick and Sam exchanged uneasy glances.

"We have a party coming in tomorrow," Mick explained, sitting on the edge of the desk. "It's a big party, and a booking we can't afford to lose."

It sounded good to him. "And?" he prompted.

"They're from Brazil. Some of the country's best paddlers. They want to kayak the Little White Salmon."

"What's the problem?"

"Their translator is ill with appendicitis, and he can't accompany them tomorrow. If they don't have a translator, we can't do the safety drills, explain the route, the dangers."

"We'll be forced to refund them, and we can't afford that," Sam stated, sounding grim.

"And for some of them, this is a dream trip, one they saved money for years to do," Mick added.

"And nobody in their group speaks English?" Fletch asked.

They shook their heads. "One or two of them speak enough to order lunch or hail a taxi, but not enough to get across the finer points of kayaking one of the most dangerous rivers in the world."

"Google Translate?"

"Again, it's not accurate enough," Mick gloomily stated. "And nobody in town speaks Portuguese. We're just going to have to cancel and take the hit."

Mick pulled his phone out of his pocket, his face as long as a Siberian winter's night, and Fletch shook his head. "Hold on, I think I can get a translator for you."

"Seriously?" Mick asked.

"Mmm-hmm." Yep, he knew Portuguese was one of the languages Rheo spoke. And if he could get Rheo to translate, he could not only save their trip, but he could maybe restore some of her confidence in her ability to translate.

"When are they arriving?"

Mick reached for a file on his desk and flipped it open. "Tomorrow. We'll pick up the group at their hotel and be at the river by six. If you could find us a translator, we'd owe you big, and give you reduced rates for the rest of the season."

Fletch laughed. "There's no need to go that far," he said. "Let me talk to my friend and I'll give you a call. Probably within the next hour."

Fletch headed home—when did he start thinking of the Pink House as home?—considering how best to approach Rheo.

She'd say yes, of course she would. It was a simple job and a good way for her to dip her toe back into face-to-face translating.

"No."

Rheo looked at Fletch, horrified at his suggestion.

No way could she translate a safety briefing, not when

people's lives were at stake. What if she made a mistake and told them to go left when they should go right? What if she told them to slow down when they should speed up? She knew nothing about kayaking!

"Absolutely not," Rheo stated, drying her hands on a kitchen towel. She'd just finished wiping the surfaces of the kitchen cabinets, a delaying tactic to avoid another translating module. There was nothing she wanted to do less.

Except translate for a group of Brazilian kayakers.

"If you don't, their holiday will be ruined and they will have wasted their time and money," Fletch said, putting his hands on her hips.

God, she loved it when he touched her, loved his big hands on her body. Sex with Fletch was a mind-blowing experience. Some nights his passion flirted on the sexy edge of kink; at others he slowed down, taking his time and delaying their intense orgasms. She never knew what to expect—a quickie in the living room or hours of concentrated lovemaking— and trying to work out Fletch's mood distracted her from her increasingly worrying life-work situation.

Fletch brushed her hair off her face, his smile soft and encouraging. "Do you speak Portuguese, Rheo?"

She shrugged. "Yes."

"On a scale of one to ten, how fluent are you?"

She wrinkled her nose. "Probably a six."

"Because you have a habit of underestimating your talents, I'm taking that as an eight. Have you done any Portuguese-to-English translations at the UN?"

"I'm in the Spanish section, Fletch," Rheo told him, seeing his trap and trying to avoid it.

Fletch just lifted one eyebrow, a demand for her to answer his question. At times like this, she caught glimpses of the expedition leader: cool, calm, and focused. He wasn't going to let her avoid the question.

"I've translated Portuguese before," she reluctantly admitted, "but it was ages ago!"

"If it's good enough for the UN, it's good enough for the kayakers. Stop being a wuss, Rheo, and do this for them. Two Gilmartin guides, friends of mine, are going to lose a shit ton of money if they don't pull this off."

Arrgh! Rheo tossed her hands in the air, feeling like a bitch for saying no. Fletch made it sound so easy—just stand there and translate the words. But if she got it wrong, there could be real-world repercussions.

"They are experienced kayakers, Rheo," Fletch said, reading her mind. "They would've attended many, many safety briefings and watched countless videos of the run. The safety briefing must happen because (a) it's a good thing to do and (b) for legal cover, so they'll know if you say something that doesn't sound right. They'll ask for clarification. You're making more of this than what it should be."

Rheo thought back to when her words disappeared as she translated for the Spanish trade minister, and the moisture in her mouth dried up. "But what happens if all my words go poof again?"

Fletch shook his head, his face showing no hint of doubt. "They won't, Rhee. Trust yourself."

So much harder to do than he thought. Fletch, having

climbed mountains and hacked his way through jungles, trekked through blizzards, and solo-climbed sheer rock walls, did not doubt himself. Rheo wished for a smidgen of his self-confidence.

"Your words won't disappear, and you will be fine," Fletch told her, bending his head to kiss her on the ticklish spot where her neck met her jaw. "We'll leave here at four."

She jerked back, her eyes wide. "In the *morning*?"

"No, in the afternoon, because the run takes a few hours, and they want to do it when it's dark."

She narrowed her eyes at his sarcasm. "I don't *do* mornings," she told him. Why would she want to leave her nice, warm, comfortable bed at such a ludicrous hour? Fletch rolled his eyes and she relented. "Okay, okay! I'll go into town, do the briefing, and come back to bed."

Fletch's mouth twitched with amusement. "The briefing will be at the river, at least an hour's drive from here," he told her.

Rheo sighed. Of course it was. "I'm not good early in the morning," Rheo told Fletch, thinking he needed the warning. "I haven't started my transition from swamp witch to human yet."

He grinned. "I've seen you at that time of the morning and you aren't that scary, Rheo Whitlock."

Ha! Maybe not, but then again, he kissed her awake to make love to her, not to boot her out of bed to go adventuring. It was a very different set of circumstances...

Rheo had told the truth: she was dreadful early in the morning when sex wasn't on the table. She'd bitched when he shook her awake and complained bitterly about being forced to find clothes and brush her teeth at an hour that, she told him three or four times, was only fit for psychopaths and lunatics. He encouraged her to drink lots of coffee while he drove her to the river, and she slowly transformed from grump to gorgeous girl.

But, as she'd told him, so much coffee made her need to pee, and he saw her mood plummet when he informed her that her only option was to go behind a tree. After splashing water on her hands, she approached the excited group and dredged up a smile for Mick and Sam, gradually thawing under their effusive thanks.

She still wasn't happy with him. Fletch wasn't fazed—she'd return to normal sooner or later.

Sitting on a log, his long legs stretched out in front of him, Fletch listened as Rheo translated for Mick, her speech becoming more rapid and her tone more confident as time passed. He wished he was preparing to kayak the river, but he'd promised Carrie he'd wait for her. He could do anything else, Carrie told him, but she wanted them to kayak the Little White Salmon together. But, damn, his friend was taking her time to get here. On the plus side, the longer Carrie stayed away, the more time he got with Rheo...

Fletch sipped from his thermos cup, enjoying the good hot coffee. Mick and Sam provided flasks of coffee and packed breakfast for their clients, and they'd tossed in provisions for him and Rheo. There was nothing better than hot coffee, a river running behind him, and the sound of birds informing each other they'd survived the night.

Laughter from the kayakers drifted over to him. Rheo looked delighted that she'd made them laugh, and he smiled when she replied to one of the younger kayaker's quips. She looked happy and confident. He could easily imagine her working at the UN, dressed in a business suit, her hair tamed and her concentration fierce as she listened, translated, and listened some more. Working with languages, and people, was her passion, just like exploring the harder, rougher, and more remote places of the Earth was his.

Pride in her bubbled up. He could see that it was as hard for her to do this as she'd feared. She'd told him about her work screwup, but something else had happened to make her so skittish. He recognized Rheo's strength and couldn't believe one incident had sent her running to a town she didn't like, forcing her to hide out in her grandmother's house.

What happened? What pushed her train off the rails? He wanted to know. Every day, his curiosity increased, and his fascination rose. It should be the other way around. Normally, by this point, he'd be bored and wanting to move on. Not necessarily to another woman but to another place and another experience. Each trip felt like a victory against his past limitations. But Rheo made him want to stay.

And stay.

Being so different, he couldn't understand their connection, which was mental as well as physical. Rheo'd told him about her life in New York City—it sounded a little bland and a little too regimented for him—and she looked horrified when he told her he'd encountered a sixteen-foot anaconda deep in the Amazon basin. If she didn't like peeing behind a bush, she'd hate camping and wouldn't survive the first day of one of his trips. In fairness, if she took him to a book reading or a ballet recital in the city, he'd be asleep within ten minutes.

Opposites supposedly attracted, but Fletch and Rheo were an extreme case. Luckily, they accepted their relationship couldn't go anywhere. There was no chance of anything permanent. He didn't do forever, and Rheo had enough issues with her adventurous family without her adding an explorer lover to the list. No, they both understood their time together at the Pink House was an anomaly, a fracture in space and time. Like hot water on a camp stove, it wasn't destined to last.

He liked it that way...

Didn't he?

Later that morning, Rheo and Fletch sat at a window booth in Abi's diner. They were her first customers of the day and were enjoying their second breakfasts. Well, Fletch was enjoying his, but Rheo couldn't raise any enthusiasm for fresh fruit salad and unsweetened yogurt. She'd become more conscious of the weight she'd put on over the past few months, and sleeping with Fletch, whose body could make angels weep, made her more self-conscious than usual.

Oh, she wasn't fat, and Fletch loved her body—he told her so often—but him cooking healthy and tasty meals for her made her want to embrace a healthier lifestyle.

Rheo had silently vowed to start eating better and maybe getting some exercise. She'd even looked at some workout videos on YouTube, thinking she'd try one when Fletch next left the house. *Ser pan comido.* It should be a cinch. Millions did it all the time. They had to be easier and more fun than they looked.

Rheo speared a strawberry and lifted it to her lips, wishing she'd ordered pancakes loaded with nuts and chocolate syrup. Why couldn't loads of carbs be healthy? Why did the good stuff taste like crap? Why couldn't she crave carrots? These were deeply important questions to which she'd never get an answer.

"I'm going to rebuild the gazebo in the garden."

Rheo lowered her strawberry. "Why?" she asked, taking in his out-of-the-blue statement.

Sorting out the gazebo was on her to-do list. She'd made a note to have the wood removed. She'd buy her grandmother a bottle of her favorite perfume as an apology gift. If Paddy ever forgave her… Her grandmother wasn't the forgiving sort. She didn't give second chances, especially if she believed she'd been lied to. The fact that she still wasn't talking to Rheo's father, Ed, after more than a year was testament to that.

Not telling Paddy she was living in her house would be, in her grandmother's books, a pretty big offense.

Fletch loaded his fork, lifted it to his mouth, and chewed. "I like to build stuff, and I'm terrified you'll rebuild it on your own. You're crap at woodwork."

A fair assessment of her carpentry skills. "I agree. I'll stick to languages," she told him. She rested her forearms on the table and wrinkled her nose. "I'm pretty exhausted. You owe me for making me get up so early."

"Thank you for doing it." He smiled at her. "You were great today. I'm seriously impressed."

Rheo swore her insides lit up like Christmas lights. When had she last heard she was amazing? Paddy occasionally praised her as a kid, but not anymore. As Paddy informed her, adults shouldn't need constant validation.

"It wasn't half as hard as I thought it would be," Rheo admitted.

"Anticipation is always worse than the actual event," he said. "The river is never as deep and scary, the mountain never as hard, the blizzard never as cold as you think." He shook his head. "Actually, the blizzard I experienced on the Antarctic Plateau was fucking cold. There's nothing worse than trying to erect a tent in a howling wind when it's minus sixty."

"I'd just collapse and let the polar bears eat me."

"There aren't any polar bears in Antarctica," Fletch informed her, smiling.

"You know what I mean," Rheo muttered, as the doorbell above the diner's door jingled, indicating the arrival of another early-morning customer.

Fletch grinned at her, and he took a long time to pull his eyes away from hers. She knew he was remembering the hot sex they'd had in the shower last night, or maybe he was thinking of another position for them to try later.

It was a revelation to discover how much she loved sex, the act of giving and receiving pleasure. Fletch was an incredible lover, and she was far better than she was before. Less self-conscious and not so uptight.

Naked or clothed, she loved looking at him, and could do it for the longest time. His face was rugged, but intelligence sparked in his eyes. He fascinated her. If he were anyone other than a nomadic explorer, she might think she was falling for him…just a little.

Fletch looked away, and Rheo followed his gaze. Abi stood next to their table, a loaded kid's size waffle in her hands. Abi whipped away Rheo's fruit salad and dumped the plate in front of her.

"Nobody comes into my diner and plays with their food," Abi told her.

Her friend instructed Fletch to scoot up, and when he did, she sat opposite Rheo and placed her folded arms on the table. "Why are you awake so early, Whitlock? You feeling all right?"

Rheo told Fletch to explain and attacked her waffle, groaning when the combination of the crispy base, toasty nuts, and dark chocolate hit her tongue. Fletch told her about their morning and Rheo met Abi's curious gaze.

"So, does this mean you're ready to go back to work?" Abi demanded. "And are you over that hot-mic, viral-video thing?"

Rheo widened her eyes at her, and Abi winced. She, like Carrie, spoke first and thought later.

"How's the waffle?" she asked Rheo, trying to recover. "They're good, right?"

Rheo appreciated her attempt at distraction. She cut off a small bite and held out her fork to Fletch. "Try it. I guarantee it's the best waffle you'll ever taste."

Fletch took the fork and chewed. He agreed it was excellent as he pushed his empty plate to the side. "What hot-mic thing?" he asked.

Damn, he wasn't easily distracted. Abi lifted her eyebrows, silently asking whether Rheo would explain. She didn't have to—Fletch wasn't entitled to her secrets. She'd told him more about her past than he'd told her about his...

Oh, he'd talked about the funny and not-so-funny things that happened on his many trips, and enthralled her with his descriptions of far-flung places. He was always, *always* interesting to listen to. But she didn't know why he'd chosen this life, why he did what he did, and what pushed him into a transient, nomadic life. She knew nothing about his childhood.

She wasn't an open book, but he was an impenetrable vault.

"Just tell him, Rhee," Abi said.

Rheo flushed, embarrassed. She'd not only humiliated herself, she'd dragged her boss and the UN Translation Services under a hot, uncomfortable spotlight.

"Well?" Fletch asked, leaning forward. "Are you going to tell me or not?"

"Yeah, are you going to tell him or not, Rheo?" Abi demanded, clearly enjoying their battle of wills.

Rheo glared at her. Whose side was she on?

"It's not a big deal," Abi told her. "Maybe if he sees it, he'll agree, and you can relax a little."

Fat chance of that happening.

Fletch tapped his finger against his coffee mug, clearly impatient. Rheo, annoyed with him and with Abi, accessed the viral video on her phone and handed her phone to Fletch.

Rheo didn't need to see the clip; it was burned into her memory. During a break in the General Assembly meeting, the cameras in the rotunda filmed the speaker, quietly talking to her aide. There was no noise until her voice, ten seconds in, came through the speakers, crystal clear.

"The damned idiots! Jesus, this isn't rocket science. The planet is dying. Why can't we agree on that? Anyone who denies climate change exists is a grade-A asshole in my book, What? What's wrong? Oh shit!"

If Fletch smiled even a little, she'd stab him between the eyes with her fork. He wasn't allowed to smile while he watched the worst moment of her life, the catalyst for everything going wrong in her career.

His eyes crinkled, and Rheo tightened the grip on her fork. "So, how did it happen?" he asked, passing her phone back.

Rheo gestured to Abi to explain.

"When translating, Rheo works in a soundproof booth. She was the lead translator on that day. The chair spoke in Spanish, Rheo translated into English, and the other translators translated from English to French, or English to Arabic…got it?"

Fletch nodded.

"When an interpreter is not actively translating, you're supposed to switch the mic off," Abi explained.

"And Rheo didn't," Fletch said. He shrugged and looked at Rheo. "You were right though. Climate denier politicians are a bunch of assholes."

Rheo groaned. "Yeah, but you can see how insulting UN General Assembly members wasn't a smart career move."

"Rheo was sanctioned," Abi told Fletch. *Too much information, Abs, thanks.* "That's translating speak for saying she was disciplined, but they never released the name of the translator. The video went viral, but no one associated it with Rheo."

"Except my boss, my boss's boss, his boss, and all my colleagues," Rheo muttered. "Nobody but them."

Abi mimed a violinist playing. "You didn't lose your job, Rheo."

No, but it did start her on a spiral of self-doubt. The spiral widened and grew until she could barely function. And the more she tried to control her perfect, placid, and predictable life, the more the spiral intensified, turning into a whirlwind, then a tornado. Eventually, anxiety and self-doubt caused a crippling paralysis, enough to make her blank out on her next important assignment.

"I'm sorry, Rheo," Fletch told her, placing his hand on hers. He rubbed the inside of her wrist with his thumb. "You don't like being out of control or failing, do you?"

"Does anyone?" she asked, trying to be flippant and missing it by a mile.

Abi left the booth and bent to kiss Rheo's cheek. Her lips brushed her ear and Rheo heard Abi's instruction to talk to him, *dammit*. Rheo pushed her half-eaten waffle away. She stared out the window onto Main Street. At this early hour, the roads were empty, and lovelier for it. It was a pretty town... Not *her* town, of course, but still quaint. And charming in its own way.

"So, you got disciplined, and then what happened?"

Rheo sighed, annoyed. "How come I have to answer all your questions, but you don't answer any of mine?"

"I do," he told her, sounding firm. "Think about it."

Rheo tried to recall Fletch refusing to answer a direct question. He hadn't. He hadn't volunteered any information, but he never ignored a direct question. Damn, how annoying.

"What made you want to be an explorer?" she demanded. He'd opened the door and she intended to walk through.

"I spent two months in the hospital when I was fifteen and was housebound for another nine. I escaped into books about expeditions and adventurers, real and fictional. I vowed I would explore the world one day, and nothing would hold me back."

Oh…oh, *wow*. Fletch was so vital, energy crackled off him, and she couldn't imagine him being sick for so long, living without any spark.

"Did you have cancer?" she quietly asked.

He shook his head. "I got strep throat, then I developed rheumatic fever. I got over that but couldn't shake the extreme tiredness, joint and muscle pain. They eventually diagnosed me with chronic fatigue syndrome."

He rubbed his jaw, then the back of his neck. "When I was sick with CFS, I felt confined and hemmed in, by where I lived, my staid parents, and my illness. I promised myself I'd never be that person again. I developed a profound need to chase freedom and to see what was over the horizon."

Fletch lifted his coffee mug, sipped, and his piercing stare pinned her to her seat. "My turn… So, what happened after you were disciplined?"

He wasn't letting this go. "I choked, I guess. I started overthinking and overanalyzing, and I couldn't put it behind me. How can I make you understand?" She hesitated, trying to find an analogy that worked. "Have you had a cracked tooth?"

He nodded.

"Your tongue keeps going to it, right? That's how it was with me. I kept niggling at it, and the more attention I gave my mistakes, the more I screwed up. Anything and everything made me second-guess myself, and my work suffered. I was corrected twice during a live translating session, was weepy, and couldn't concentrate."

"But why did you flame out so quickly? How did you go from making a few mistakes to needing to take six months off? I'm curious about your lack of… I don't want to upset or offend you…"

After all this, she could take it. Her hide was marginally thicker these days. "Go on."

"I'm wondering why you weren't more resilient, why you couldn't accept the mistake and shrug it off. Why couldn't you learn from it and move on?"

Rheo thought she might as well tell him. Maybe if she explained it to him, it would make more sense to her.

"It's because I don't make mistakes," she replied. She waved her hands in the air when she noticed his frown. "I'm not perfect, that's not what I'm saying. I plan my life to ensure I make as few mistakes as possible, and when I do mess up, the mistakes aren't big ones. I've spent a lot of time formulating the life I want, working out the steps, the desired outcomes, how to climb over or skirt any obstacles in my way."

"That's a project management plan, not a life."

Precisely. And it worked.

"If I know what to expect, what comes next, then I don't make mistakes." Rheo dropped her shoulders and rolled them back, trying to ease the tension in her tight muscles. "Also, when you live a rigid life, when you do what is expected of you, live a life in a certain way, you don't have to cope with the unexpected. I don't like the unexpected. I find it extremely stressful."

Rheo played with the leather and copper bracelets on Fletch's strong wrist. "Our childhoods made us who we were. You felt hemmed in. I was given too much freedom, and my childhood was nomadic and unstable. My parents, like you, thrive on the unexpected."

"While my life is exciting, a lot of what I do is carefully planned. While it looks like I—and my crew—take huge risks, we've calculated the odds, and they're heavily in favor of us succeeding. I don't have a death wish, Rheo."

Maybe not, but he did spend most of his time dancing with nature, and everyone knew how tempestuous and fickle she could be.

"Thank God for Paddy. I went to live with her when I started high school. I look up to her a lot. She was, is, demanding and has high standards. She fully supported my dreams for a stable life, a different life from my parents'."

"Keep talking, Rhee. I like listening to you."

Okay then. "After making me promise I would use my education and that I wouldn't follow in my parents' footsteps, Paddy paid for me to go to college. Her firstborn son was the perfect one, a lawyer who wanted to get into politics, but he died young. She wanted her other sons to be lawyers, doctors, engineers, and didn't bank on getting a missionary and a wanderer."

"How do your parents fund their lifestyle?" Fletch asked, stroking the inside of her wrist. "It's not easy to earn money when your life is spent on the road."

As she knew. Her mom and dad had joined the van-life movement before the age of digital nomads, internet entrepreneurs, and online selling. "They bartered and traded, and my dad took odd jobs and my mom sold generic landscape paintings on street corners. I presume they are still doing much of the same."

But what would they do when they got too old to flit about? If Paddy was to be believed, they were banking on an inheritance from her. That might happen, but there was a good chance Rheo would have to rent a place for them and pay their bills when they were old. She'd tried to talk to them about their retirement plans once, ages ago, but Ed and Gail lived in the present and paid no attention to the future.

"The van-life movement is so different now than it was when your folks started," Fletcher commented. "It's still a pretty cool life though."

"As you should know," she stated, wincing at the shrill note in her voice. "You live in a van, right?"

Fletcher's eyes cooled and his voice hardened. "Did you do some internet research, Rheo?" he asked, his tone silky but cold. "And, for accuracy, I live in a tiny house."

"It's on wheels, right?" Rheo pulled her hand away from his and leaned back. "You can pick it up and move wherever the hell you want to go."

She knew she sounded bitter and resentful. Fletch had the right to own what he wanted, live life the way he wanted to... She knew that, she *did*. But every similarity between him and her parents was the swing of a wrecking ball through her soul. Connections between them dredged up her insecurities and had her wanting to check the eviction clause on her lease and the balance on her savings accounts to make sure none of her money was missing. That the world was the right way forward.

"Currently, my house, all 350 square feet of it, sits at the end of a friend's massive property. I rent the land from him because I don't see the point of owning a property and paying taxes on it when I'm never there."

Rheo rubbed her fingers across her forehead, feeling caught out and clumsy. Her parents and their source of income—along with her father's demand to see Paddy's will—were her nuclear hot buttons.

Should she apologize? She caught the annoyance in Fletch's eyes and decided not to add fuel to the fire. But, damn, was speaking without thinking something she did now?

The waitress walked over, handed him the bill, and took his card. She swiped it, frowned, and sent Fletch a pained smile. "I'm so sorry, sir, there seems to be a problem with your card."

Fletch took his card back, puzzled. Embarrassed for him, Rheo touched his hand with her fingers. "I left my wallet at home, so I can't pay, but Abi will let me pay later."

He flipped it over and looked at the date. "It's not expired. Why isn't it working?"

"You probably missed a payment, or you've maxed it out."

Fletch's hot glare held enough heat to burn her to a crisp. What? If it walked like a duck, talked like a duck…

"Thanks for that."

Oh God, he sounded pissed. Fletch flipped open his wallet, took out some cash, and handed it over with a hefty tip. He smiled at the waitress, who looked as uncomfortable as Rheo felt.

"There you go," he told her.

She smiled and nodded. "No problem, Mr. Wright. Thanks for the tip."

Fletch stood and looked at Rheo, his expression remote.

Shit, why had she said that? She'd insulted his living arrangements and then made assumptions about his finances. This was what happened when she delved into her past, when she allowed it to mess with her head. Where Fletch lived and how he managed his money had nothing to do with her.

Rheo got to her feet and tucked her phone into the back pocket of her jeans. Fletch waited for her to proceed, but Rheo told him she'd see him outside, as she wanted to say goodbye to Abi.

Rheo scuttled around the counter to where Abi stood.

"Why is Fletch looking like a rattlesnake bit him in the balls, Rhee?" her friend demanded, keeping her voice low.

"Oh, he's pissed because his credit card was declined. I offered to arrange for him to pay you later. He paid in cash."

"Still doesn't explain why he's pissed," Abi murmured. "What did you say?"

She rocked on her heels. "I might've said something about it being maxed out or him not making a payment on time."

"Dear God, Rheo, who gave you permission to be let out on your own?" Abi muttered, shaking her head.

Rheo waved her words away. "Oh, please, it happens occasionally for everyone, but more often with people like *him*!"

Abi slapped her hands on her hips. "He's a semi-famous documentary maker, Rheo. He's not Bear Grylls, but he's not a drifter!"

Rheo groaned and lifted her crossed arms to cover her eyes. "I know, I know!" She lowered her arms and pushed the heels of her hands into her eye sockets. "Okay, maybe my reaction was pure reflex, because it happened so often with my parents. Honestly, I was always shocked if the charge went through the first time."

"I think you're being seriously judgmental, Whitlock! Maybe there's simply an issue with his card, and it got rejected. Shit like that happens...*all the time*."

Yes, she accepted that. "But I also understand people who chase freedom, Abi. The people I met on the road lived a hand-to-mouth existence, and they paid no attention to their finances. All that was important was what was over the horizon. He's a nice guy, but I don't think we can be anything other than bed buddies," she told Abi, ignoring the surge of disappointment flooding her system. "I could never be with someone who doesn't have a backup plan, someone with no savings, who can't budget."

Abi's eyes widened. "Oh my God, you are *such* a snob!"

No, she wasn't. She simply understood her levels of tolerance. She couldn't handle someone who wasn't financially responsible. Things like this hurtled her back to the insecurity of her childhood, as evidenced by her reaction to his card not going through. Fletch was a great lover, but he'd be a disastrous boyfriend or long-term partner.

"I'll talk to you later," she told Abi, not wanting to argue anymore.

They might connect on many levels, and Rheo adored her, but Abi didn't understand how every cell in her body rebelled against her parents' free-spirited way of life. To someone who liked coloring inside the lines, their—and Fletch's—lifestyle was terrifying.

Nine

Rheo walked out of the diner and joined Fletch on the sidewalk. She clocked his rigid expression and sighed. He was still pissed. She felt her skin prickle and her hackles rise—maybe she had spoken out of turn and come across as harsh, but the the main reason credit cards didn't work was because they were maxed out. It wasn't like she'd suggested he was a kitten kicker.

Rheo turned to walk home but Fletch's hand on her elbow stopped her. He pulled out his phone and waved it. "Give me a minute. I want to check what's going on with my card."

Her early-morning start was catching up with her, and she wanted to go home for a nap. Going back to work and putting in an eight- to ten-hour day was going to kick her ass. Her sabbatical had made her soft and lazy.

Fletch rested his back against the wall between Abi's shop and the boutique next door and lifted his boot, placing his foot on the wall behind him. His fingers flew over his phone and Rheo went to stand beside him, a fair distance away so she couldn't see his screen and invade his privacy. He punched buttons, cursed softly, and punched more buttons.

"Everything is fine. My card must be faulty," he told her.

Rheo wanted to believe him, but she'd heard the excuse a hundred times. She would far prefer him to be honest.

Admittedly, with this credit card situation and his reaction, she'd lost a little respect for him. Relief rolled through her. There was no way she would fall for him now. This was an insurmountable barrier, and even if he had another occupation, if he was a banker or accountant or lawyer, she couldn't fall for a guy who, in his midthirties, didn't know how to manage his finances. Not that she'd ever had intentions of falling for him but, well, things happened.

"Jesus, I'm so close to calling it right now," Fletch told her.

Rheo frowned. What did he mean?

"I'm not crazy about people who assume shit." Fletch machine-gunned his words.

Oh. He meant *calling* whatever they had. Ending it. Rheo swayed on her feet. Okay. *Wow.*

She lifted her chin. "What shit did I assume?"

"That I am some financially challenged moron who can't find his ass with a flashlight." Before she could think of a response to his furious statement, Fletch thrust his phone at her and she looked at the screen. Her eyes darted over the information. He didn't owe any money on his credit card. In fact, he had a far bigger credit limit than hers.

Rheo started thinking she'd grabbed the wrong end of a poison-tipped stick. *Shitshitshitshit.*

"Would you like to see what I have in my bank account?" he demanded, now properly angry.

Oh crap. She'd misread this situation. Badly.

"I can assure you it's equally healthy. I also have long-term savings, a retirement plan, a healthy portfolio of stocks, shares, and cryptocurrency. I own a production company, Rheo. I'm not rolling in cash, but I make decent money."

Damn. Fuck. Rheo wrinkled her nose and met his eyes. She could talk her way out of this by lying or changing the subject, but both actions were beneath her. She'd made assumptions. And a complete ass of herself.

"I'm sorry," she said, because she had no idea what else to say.

Fletch shook his head. "Not good enough. Do you want to tell me why you assumed I'm a deadbeat traveler with no clue about how to manage my finances?"

No, she didn't. Her heart stumbled around her chest, and a lead weight sat in her stomach. She'd hurt him—she could see pain under his irritated expression, in the frostiness of his eyes. Hot shame and cold remorse made her body temperature irregular.

A truck slid into the parking space a few yards from them, and another car slid into one farther up. Gilmartin was waking up, and she didn't want to beg forgiveness on the sidewalk.

She placed her hand on his arm and Rheo winced when he yanked it away. "If I have to explain—"

"Oh, you do," Fletch assured her.

"Then can I do it at home?"

He stared at her, obviously debating whether to demand an answer right now or whether he could wait. Fletch eventually nodded, turned, and walked in the direction of the Pink House.

Rheo half ran to match his long-legged stride, and she was puffing by the time they reached the gate of the Pink House.

"You could've slowed down," she complained as they walked around the house to enter the kitchen via the back door.

Fletch ignored her, standing back after opening the door for her. "Look, I'm too pissed to have a rational conversation with you right now. I'll find you when I'm ready," Fletch informed her and stomped back out the door.

Right. *Shit.*

A few hours later, in the Pink House's empty kitchen, Fletch leaned against the counter by the coffee machine and crossed his arms. He was still seriously pissed off and had been since Rheo made her comments about him living in a van. Somewhere along the line, she'd assumed he'd stumbled from country to country, living hand-to-mouth. That she hadn't looked further, or asked him, annoyed him even more.

And her ability to piss him off pissed him off *more*. He cared far too much about her and her opinion. He never gave a crap about how people viewed him; he didn't spend a moment worrying about shit like that. People either liked him or didn't, accepted him or didn't.

He *did* care what Rheo thought…

Fuck. Not good.

Fletch reached for an apple from the fruit bowl and crunched down. He was—cliché or not—a lone wolf and had been for most of his life. His parents weren't overly involved. Their aim was to make themselves superfluous to him as early as possible and insisted on him becoming independent from a young age. They never did anything for him he couldn't do himself, and it made him self-sufficient. But there had also been a level of disengagement between them, and he carried that detachment into the other relationships in his life.

CFS had made him feel vulnerable, a sharp contrast to the independence instilled in him by his parents, and he avoided relationships that required him to expose his vulnerabilities. He had friends, like Carrie, Seb, and the senior members of his crew, but he didn't easily let people in. Few people knew he had his own production company and that his company owned the rights to his adventure documentaries, as well as producing other travel shows. He left the day-to-day running of the company to his capable CEO and staff. In his industry, despite him owning a tiny house and wearing old jeans, he was a success.

He only ever indulged in brief sexually charged relationships and never allowed anything serious to develop. Falling for someone was something he refused to do, because commitment would limit his freedom and tie him down. He was close-ish to Carrie, but that was only because she chased freedom as hard as he did, and there wasn't a dash of chemistry between them.

Rheo rapped on the door frame of the kitchen. She'd

showered and pulled on a short flower-print sundress. She stood on one bare foot, the other tucked behind her calf. Rheo's blue eyes met his and her remorse dropped his anger a notch. But she wasn't off the hook yet, not nearly. He still needed, and deserved, an explanation.

"Can I come in?"

He nodded and continued to eat his apple. She pulled a chair from beneath the wooden table and sat. "As I mentioned, my parents lived in a van before it became a thing," Rheo explained. "I lived with them until I went to high school."

"You make it sound like they sentenced you to ten years in a penal colony," Fletcher coldly stated. "A lot of people would consider yours a fantastic childhood."

She pulled a face. "I hated every minute of it," she told him.

He heard the crack in her voice and his attention sharpened.

"I hated not knowing where we were, where we were going, or what it would look like when we got there. I hated the changing view. We often broke down. And because we lived on top of each other, I heard every discussion between my parents and listened to them fighting about money, how little they had and how to get more. They were always short. It didn't help that they were into fishing and hiking and rock climbing while I hated getting dirty and sweaty, and I have a fear of heights."

Fletch tossed his core in the trash and sat opposite her. To a teen with CFS, hers sounded like the dream childhood—

everything he wanted to do all the time. But he could admit that if Rheo didn't enjoy the lifestyle, if she craved security and stability, if she hated what her parents loved—and it sounded like she did—then living in a van would've been hell.

But he still didn't understand how her past related to her assumptions about his financial status.

"Why did you make those assumptions about me? Because of your parents?"

Rheo looked away, her focus on the marks left on the wooden table by countless Pink House dinners. "My parents are useless with money. Their old van is held together by duct tape and prayers, and I have no idea how they manage to afford to keep it and themselves on the road. I witnessed money sliding through their hands. You live in a tiny house, you don't wear fancy clothes, we'd just been talking about them…and when your credit card was declined—"

He sighed. "You thought I was like them."

"It was a gut reaction…and so wrong of me. I'm sorry." She did look mortified, and he knew she was sorry.

But he needed more. "Were your parents that bad or did your childish imagination make it worse than it was?"

Kids had a way of exaggerating; he'd done it himself. Some days he thought his nine months spent dragging his tired ass around was the teenage equivalent of being a prisoner. Other days he thought they weren't bad, just deeply boring. It depended on his mood and emotional buoyancy.

"I don't know," Rheo replied, lifting her shoulders to her ears.

His parents had taught him to be independent, but they'd also distanced themselves from his emotional needs. He found it difficult to form bonds. He tended to keep everyone at arm's length, and it came at the cost of a deeper connection. This was the first time in—well, shit—forever that he wanted to dive deeper. He needed to get to the bottom of this. He needed to understand. Understand *her*. To do that, he needed more information.

"Tell me about them, Rhee."

"My parents? What more can I say?"

Rheo looked off into the distance and he waited her out. She would either talk or not. He would wait till later to work out why he was going against the habits of a lifetime to learn everything about her.

Much, much later.

"I'm more like Paddy than like them. She's organized and thoughtful, and she's an incredible planner. As I said, I came to live with her when I was thirteen, and my world, for the first time, made sense. I had a routine, a bed that didn't move, and a view that didn't change. I was so grateful to feel settled that I emulated her in every way I could. Paddy planned, so I planned. Paddy read and spoke languages, so I did the same. She's been my role model and I'm terrified of disappointing her. When she finds out how I screwed up and had to take a sabbatical and that I've been living here—"

The moisture in her eyes suggested she was getting emotional. "Take a breath, Rheo."

"—she's going to lose her shit. And Paddy losing her shit is not a fun experience."

"Aren't you overreacting?"

"I wish I was," Rheo replied, sounding glum. "Paddy has higher expectations for me than she does for the rest of the family. I'm like her, the one who's living life the way it should be lived."

Right, she was back to sounding judgmental. There was more than one way of living life, but Paddy, and her granddaughter, had obviously missed that memo.

"People have a right to live the way they want to, Rheo."

"Paddy doesn't believe that, but I do," Rheo agreed. "But you have to be able to pay for the life you lead."

Fletch scratched the side of his neck and made the connection. "And your parents didn't do that?"

"No, while they lived very frugal lives, they still never made enough money to pay for their way of life. Instead of doing something else, *anything* else, they borrowed money from family and friends, frequently 'forgetting' to pay them back. And if the demands for repayment got too loud, they borrowed money from someone else to repay that loan, with a little extra, and the snake started to eat its tail."

"Did they borrow money from you?"

Rheo nodded. "More times than I can recall. I worked through high school and college so I had money to send them. They promised to repay it at the end of the week, the end of the month. Then they stopped making promises. Months would pass, they'd ask for another loan, and the cycle started again. Eventually, I just accepted I'd never get the money back. Love was tainted with resentment, respect with disappointment."

"Something else happened." He knew there was more to her story. "What else happened?"

Rheo threw her hands up, bemused. "How do you see what I don't want you to?"

Easy to answer. "I keep telling you, you have an exceptionally expressive face. What else pissed you off?"

"You are so persistent," she complained.

"If I wasn't, I wouldn't do what I do. Spill."

Rheo traced a crack in the table with the edge of her thumbnail. "My father borrowed quite a bit of money from Paddy. He promised her, faithfully, hand on his heart, he'd repay it. I had my doubts and so did Paddy. He didn't pay it back." Rheo wrinkled her nose. "During one of their arguments, my father demanded to see Paddy's will. He wanted to know what he was going to inherit from her. She was furious and refused to talk to him until he apologized for being so crass and greedy."

"And did he?"

"He admitted to asking her about her will, checking that she had one and that her affairs were in order. He insists he never asked to *see* her will."

It sounded like a special type of bullshit to him, and they all needed their heads knocked together.

"I know it sounds ridiculous, Fletch, it *is* ridiculous," Rheo told him, rubbing her hands over her face. "But you can predict future behavior by past behavior. My parents have never saved, and they are getting older, and even my Peter Pan parents have to, at some point, start thinking of the future. The easiest way to fund their future is through inheriting money from Paddy. Paddy's pissed because she worked damn hard for the money she'll leave behind, and my parents, in her eyes, haven't worked at all. She feels my father is being dishonest because he won't admit to asking to see her will."

"But you're being deceitful too," Fletch pointed out. "And you're being a little hypocritical too. Aren't you?"

He expected her to argue, but she didn't. "Because I haven't told Paddy I'm living here and what happened at work? Of course I am." Misery jumped in and out of Rheo's eyes.

Points for being self-aware, Rheo. But, man, her family situation was complicated, dominated by strong characters, misunderstandings, and undercurrents. He wasn't into drama, thanks. It was another bullet point to add to his don't-get-involved-with-Rheo list.

He was only here for another few weeks and wasn't sure how long Rheo would be around either. The link between them was great sex and enjoying each other's company. So God knew why he was asking about her family and digging into her past and problems. He needed to stop that shit. Immediately.

To distract himself, he shifted his thoughts to the way she made him feel physically. Rheo seemed to love sex as much as he did, and there wasn't a better form of distraction. And they needed to be distracted, needed to be yanked out of the emotional and into the sexual.

Fletch walked around the table and held out his hand to Rheo. He wrapped his arms around her body, thinking about how well she fit next to his, how they seemed to be made for each other. Her soft against his hard, her femininity a perfect complement to his brawn. He slid his hand under her shirt, needing her hot, soft, fragrant skin under his hand. He brushed his mouth across hers and lifted his head to look at her.

"We talk far too much," he told her, wondering if she'd get the subtext behind his comment. The more they talked, the closer they got, and that was dangerous. For him. For her. They needed to dissolve the emotionally sticky web they'd run into.

Awareness flashed and her nod came quickly. "We should definitely *do* more and talk less," she told him, running the tips of her fingers along his jaw.

They were thinking alike, thank God. Relieved, Fletch covered her mouth with his, loving the way she responded, with no hesitation.

Rheo's tongue tangled around his in a hot, slick slide, and her kiss annihilated thoughts of anything but the way she made him hum, then burn. Fletch swiped his thumb across her already hard nipple, waiting for her groan. Fletch sensed, no ego involved, he was the best lover she'd had. It was a title he was proud to own.

Fletch lifted her and sat her on the wooden kitchen table, shoving her skirt up her legs to bunch it across the top of her thighs. She spread her legs and he touched the wet spot on her plain white cotton panties. "I love how responsive you are," Fletch said, his voice a growl.

"Lift your ass," he told her.

Rheo lifted, and he pulled her panties down her legs, dropping them to the table next to her bare thigh. He looked down at her, open to his gaze, all pink and pretty and swollen and wet.

"Gorgeous. I can't wait to be inside you."

Rheo clasped the back of his head and pulled him down, feeding him hot, want-you, open-mouth kisses. He knew what she was trying to say: *Take me away, make me stop thinking, get me out of my head...*

She wanted his fingers, his mouth, and his cock in her, over her, taking and filling her.

He'd give her what she desired...eventually.

Fletch pushed her dress's thin straps down her arms, and the top fell to join the skirt in a bunch around her hips. He unhooked her plain white bra and immediately fastened his mouth on her nipple, sucking it to the roof of his mouth. Her hand held his head in place, and he heard her soft pants, and her skin felt hotter. Her smell—the sexy, musky smell of perfume and a turned-on woman—hit his nose and his cock pushed against the fabric of his shorts, painfully hard. Needing more, he switched to her other breast, and teased her with his teeth before pulling her dress over her head and tossing it to the floor.

As long as he lived, he'd remember Rheo sitting on her grandmother's table, the morning sun streaming into the room, painting her skin with a rose-gold sheen. He hooked a finger under the band holding up her hair and pulled it away. Her hair tumbled down her back, glinting in the sunlight.

Keeping his hands off her was nearly impossible, but he

needed to burn this image in his mind. Her breasts were
full and high, her nipples a delicious pink. Rheo placed her
hands on the table behind her and looked at him, her gaze
bold and confident. As his eyes moved down her body, over
her rounded stomach, she spread her legs wide. Beneath the
tidy patch of hair, her lips were pink and inviting. They glis-
tened, and Fletch licked his lips, desperate to kiss her there.

This was what he needed, what he thought she needed
too. After an argument, sex could be a reset, a way to push
feelings, complications, and irritations away, to get back to
the basics.

What did he know for sure? That they were just two con-
senting adults enjoying each other, cramming in as much
good sex as they could before life pulled them apart and sent
them in different directions.

Sex, this insane biological need to be together, made sense
when not much else did.

"Let me look at you too, Fletch," Rheo commanded him.

Unable to refuse her anything, he fumbled as he undid
the button on his pants. Within seconds, less, he was naked.
When her eyes hit his cock, he stroked his shaft from base
to tip, imagining her lips around him, taking him deep. The
wet warmth, her tongue rimming his head...

"That's hot," Rheo said, her voice breathy. "You're hot."

Rheo's hand dipped between her legs, and she dragged
her finger through her folds and swirled the tip around her
clit. Thinking was bad, watching was good, but he preferred action...

Fletch dropped to his knees and, because he was tall, found

his head was at the perfect height. He placed both his hands on the inside of her thighs, spread her wide, and covered her clit with his mouth. He licked. Then delved. Rheo moaned, then shuddered, but he didn't stop. He sucked her clit onto his tongue, then lathed it gently, changing the pressure and intensity every few seconds.

Fletch looked up into her eyes, foggy with lust, and his heart did a one-two thump. It felt too full, on the brink of exploding in his chest, less sexual, more emotional. He yanked his eyes away, not wanting her to see how she undid him, that she made him weak, how he wanted to fall apart in her arms…how he could fit into her life.

She was unlike anyone he'd ever met. Could staying in one place for her be worth it?

What was he thinking?

Why was he thinking?

Fletch felt Rhee's fingers tugging his hair, her harsh moans continuing. This was so much fun—making her come was his new favorite thing to do. It was the best way, in his opinion, to spend a morning. He lapped, sucked, stroked, and Rheo lay flat, her head tipped back and her hair spreading over the table. His hands went beneath her ass, and he lifted her, changing the angle, and pushed his tongue into her, then retreated to suck on her. Through panting breaths, she told him to put his fingers inside her, and he did, working in two, then three fingers. He ate at her, and she screamed, coming against his fingers and into his mouth with a hot, wet rush.

Her shaking continued as he pushed his cock into all that amazing heat and wetness. Her legs locked around his hips, and when he was as deep in her as he could go, he stopped moving. This was another moment he wanted to be burned into his memory bank.

"Why have you stopped?" she demanded, her voice ragged.

"Some things are meant to be savored," he replied, shocked at how unsteady his voice sounded. "And I need a condom."

"I'm on the pill and tested negative for everything at my last physical. If you did too…" She lifted her hands to cradle his face. "I need you to take me, Fletch. Hard and fast and fiercely…"

He wanted to, but he was a big guy, and she was a lot smaller than him. "I want to… God, so much."

"I can handle it, Fletch," she assured him, challenge in her deep blue eyes. "I can handle you."

God, he loved her boldness. He pulled back, nearly all the way out, and plunged back inside her, burying his cock deep, loving the delicious feel of being skin on skin with her.

Blood roared as he found her mouth, kissing her with ferocious intensity. This was wild and primal, and he imagined fucking Rheo outside next to a river on a rock under the hot, bold sun. Given how much she hated the outdoors, she'd probably hate it, and a chuckle rose up his throat. He'd never wanted to laugh during sex before.

Then again, he'd laughed more with Rheo in the last few weeks than he had in years.

He pulled back to look at her and fell into her bright blue eyes.

"Taking you is the best thing," he told her.

Rheo's eyes widened and then she smiled. One day, sometime soon, he wanted to come on her smile.

Rheo's hand slapping his ass, her rough voice demanding he make her come again, jerked him back. He'd been so inside his head, he'd lost track of his body, and her body.

That had never happened before. It wouldn't happen again.

Fletch pounded into her, his hand under her butt anchoring her to him. Rheo lifted her hips, and when she gripped him, he finally let go, pulsing inside her, five or six times, shuddering as his orgasm rocketed from his balls to the base of his skull.

"Rhee... *God*. We're *so* good at this."

And fucking awful at the rest.

He rested his face against her neck, panting softly against her skin. *Best sex ever.*

"Why am I doing this?" Rheo demanded, five minutes into their hike. She glared at Fletch's back as she followed him down a narrow path through a dense forest. She was a strong-willed woman, so how did he manage to persuade her to pull on a pair of leggings and a never-used pair of sneakers and follow him through a forest?

Sex. He'd asked her when his head was between her legs late last night, and she'd said yes. In her defense, she would've agreed to dive with great white sharks at that point. Without a cage...with chum in the water.

"You play dirty, Wright. Using sex to lure me to hike with you," Rheo complained. "I don't hike."

Fletch didn't look back, neither did he stop. "It's a walk on a trail not two miles from your house, Whitlock. News-flash…this is not an expedition to summit K2."

The man was fluent in sarcasm. Damn, she liked that about him.

Rheo looked at the huge trees, caught glimpses of the sky beyond them, and decided it wasn't, well, *bad*. In fact, it was quite pretty.

"You do realize we could be back in bed right now?"

Fletch, as she expected, ignored her. He wore a small backpack, and she prayed it contained a thermos of coffee. She needed a reward for being active. But she still maintained that sex was a more fun way to pass time.

But the air was fresh, and the sun, when it touched her face and shoulders, was toasty on her skin. She liked stretching her muscles and enjoyed the silence. No, it wasn't silent— she could hear birds chirping, a stream burbling, the crack of a branch, and the whistle of the wind. But it was peaceful. And, yes—she almost didn't want to admit it—rather lovely.

She wasn't going to tell Fletch her thoughts. If she did, she'd never hear the end of it. And if she gave him an inch, she might next find herself in a kayak or in a harness pre-paring to climb a rock face.

Rheo wound her thin sweatshirt around her hips as she recalled yesterday's fight. Embarrassment still burned. She was too old to make stupid assumptions. At her age, she should know better.

After she recovered from their hot kitchen sex—how was she ever going to enjoy family dinners knowing what she and Fletch had done on that table?—she'd apologized to Fletch again for being so judgmental. He'd nodded and only asked that she not do it again.

But she couldn't stop the niggling thought… She'd been so quick to assume the worst about him. Did she do the same thing with her family? And after talking to Fletch about her family, she questioned her attitude toward her parents. She'd simply accepted Paddy's version of her and her dad's argument about the will. Rheo never reached out to get his side of the story. She made her judgment solely based on Paddy's perceptions. She trusted her grandmother, but Paddy was intolerant and easily frustrated.

What if, like Rheo had today, Paddy got it wrong?

Her grandmother wasn't infallible—though she liked to think she was—and she was getting older. What if Rheo's dad was being honest? What if his explanation was the truth? Ed was many things—he admitted to being disorganized, lazy and unambitious—but he wasn't a liar. He preferred to avoid painful subjects rather than bring them into the open and deal with them.

Believing Paddy's version of events was easy. It was what she'd always done. Rheo *always* sided with her grandmother. They were the sensible members of the family, the ones who did things right. According to them…

People have a right to live their lives their way…

Rheo, deep in thought, crashed into Fletch and his arm encircled her, keeping her on her feet.

"Daydreaming, sweetheart? Wishing you were some-where else?"

While she was lost in her thoughts, they'd hit a stream. A simple but sturdy wooden plank bridge was the only way to cross the water.

Fletch gestured to a fallen log. "Let's sit."

Rheo sat and stretched out her legs. Ahead was a clear-ing, and in the distance, a lake. She turned at the sound of chatter behind her and watched a group of teenage girls ap-proaching them, fit and young and radiating energy. They wore expensive hiking boots, tight shorts, and crop tops. Rheo felt frumpy in her misshapen gray T-shirt and brown leggings. This pair had a hole in the fabric on the inside of her right thigh, so she kept her knees locked together.

The kids greeted them, skipped across the bridge, and strode away. Rheo, because she was fantastically mature, stuck out her tongue at their departing backs.

"It's nice to see kids in nature and not behind a screen," Fletch said, pouring hot coffee into the mug from the ther-mos. He handed it to her. "We'll have to share the mug. I didn't bring another."

Rheo sipped, thanked him, and eyed his rucksack. "Did you bring anything to eat? I'm starving."

He rolled his eyes. "Again, we are only two miles from home. You had breakfast twenty minutes ago!" he reminded her.

"Fresh air makes me hungry," she muttered.

"You really need to get out more," Fletch told her, his mouth quirking.

She loved his smile. It softened his face and made him seem more relaxed. Rheo decided to throw him a bone and used the coffee cup to gesture to the view. "This isn't terrible," she conceded.

"Be still my beating heart," he dryly replied, removing the coffee cup from her grasp, its contents sloshing over the rim. "I'll take that before you spill it."

They passed the cup back and forth, the silence comfortable. Fletch seemed happy to be quiet and let her think.

His phone buzzed and Fletch pulled it from the side pocket of his cargo shorts.

"Aren't you supposed to switch your phone off when you're out in nature?" Rheo demanded.

"Again, we're on the outskirts of Gilmartin, not in the upper reaches of the Andes," Fletch replied, opening an email. He read it and his expression, excited but hesitant, intrigued her.

"Good news?"

He put his phone away and tossed the dregs of the coffee onto the grass. "Discovery Channel wants me to host a program on what they call Lazarus species. I need to tell them whether I'm interested or not."

"What's a Lazarus species?"

"They are animals we thought were extinct but have been found, usually in very remote habitats. The Caspian horse, the Fernandina tortoise, and the Somali elephant shrew are examples."

Rheo had never heard of any of them.

"I'd have to go to the areas where the species live, help

the scientists find them, talk about how important they are and what their loss of habitat means for them."

"It would be quite different from what you do now."

"Very," Fletch agreed. "Shorter, for one. Each trip would be about three months instead of a year. I'd be able to use my degree in biology. But it would be a big departure for me, and I'd be going off-brand."

"But you'd have a far bigger audience," Rheo pointed out. She placed her hand on his shoulder. "It sounds like it's something you'd like to do."

Excitement flared in his green eyes, which then turned dense and unreadable. "Yes, no... I don't know. I've worked damn hard to get to where I am. I would be going off course if I did this."

"Or simply finding a new way through the jungle," Rheo suggested.

"And you?" Fletch asked. "What's your plan for the future?"

Ugh, just when she'd started enjoying herself in nature, just a little. But Fletch was done talking about himself, and it was her turn. Shrugging, she wrapped her arms around her bent knees. "Dunno."

"You need to come clean to your family."

That wasn't news.

"It shouldn't be this hard, right?" she asked him, leaning sideways and resting her head on his big shoulder.

"You made a mistake, Rhee." He crossed his legs at the ankles and pushed his sunglasses into his messy hair. "You are allowed to make mistakes. It's what humans do, it's how we grow."

"Have you? Made mistakes?" she asked him.

"*Fuck*, more times than you would believe. When I was younger, my ego and my determination to get everything done better and quicker caused me to make dumbass decisions. I was damn lucky none of them ended in someone getting hurt. So, what's stopping you from telling them?"

Could she tell him? Could she be that honest with him? Would he think less of her?

"Probably my ego," she said, keeping her voice low.

He placed his hand on the back of her neck and his gentle squeeze gave her the strength to continue.

"I think I'm better than them, that I'm more sensible, the adult in the room. I really don't want to admit I messed up."

She'd followed Paddy's example and picked up on her grandmother's prejudices. She and Paddy planned everything, came home to the same bed in the same place every night and made "sensible" decisions. Her parents and Carrie were irresponsible and flighty and their choices questionable. But unlike Rheo, the flighty threesome were flexible. They could maneuver when life threw them off course.

They had more freedom, while she and Paddy played within the boxes they'd created for themselves.

Fletch kissed her temple and held his head to hers, seeming to understand how little she liked herself right now. Coming face-to-face with yourself, seeing the aspects of your personality you didn't like, was agony. Doing it in front of a man you were crazy about was torturous.

Fletch moved away, bent his legs, and rested his forearms on his knees. "Can I make a suggestion?"

Rheo nodded and made a rolling gesture with her hand.

"Why don't you explain your situation to Carrie first?"

She pulled a face and Fletch sighed.

"I don't understand why you and your cousin aren't better friends. If you met each other as adults, you'd enjoy each other. She's a little wild, sure, adventurous, but she has a heart as big as the sun. And while you think you don't have an adventurous bone in your body, you are far more open to new things than you profess to be."

Rheo gasped. "How dare you!" she stated, dramatically slapping her hand on her heart. "I'm not in the least bit adventurous!"

He ignored her amateur acting. "I think you are. There is more than one type of courage, and you don't have to run around the world to have an adventurous spirit," he told her. "And Carrie is nicer than you think, and she's a damn loyal friend."

"She can't keep a secret to save her life," Rheo muttered. Carrie spoke first and thought later.

"She can," Fletch insisted. "She's kept a couple of mine."

Rheo's stomach churned and jealousy seared her throat. She hated that Carrie knew things about Fletch that she didn't. She wanted to be the keeper of his secrets, the person who knew him best. *Crap.* She was sliding down that slippery slope from attraction to *like*, and she couldn't do that. It would be a seriously stupid move.

"You need to get out of your comfort zone, Rhee."

Okay. Change of subject. "Is that why you insisted I hike with you? Because you think I'm in a rut?" she asked.

"*Again*, this isn't a hike, it's a stroll. And, yes, you need to get out of your comfort zone. You'll get your confidence back quicker if you do things that scare you."

"I don't wanna."

He ignored her. "Tell Carrie, see how she responds. Then tell your parents and your grandmother. You've got to start moving forward, sweetheart."

Again, she didn't wanna.

But he was right. She was treading water and she either needed to swim or she would sink.

Ten

The next evening, with Fletch opting to shoot pool in a bar somewhere, Rheo took the opportunity to catch up with Abi. When her friend bought the deli building with a small business loan, she had converted the second floor into an apartment and added a thin balcony just wide enough for a small table and two chairs, overlooking Main Street. It was a great spot to watch the tourists and the Gilmartin residents walking into and out of the bars and restaurants.

Abi released a contented sigh, and Rheo rolled her head to look at her. "I'm sorry for storming out on you the other day," she said.

Abi lifted her wineglass to her nose, then took a healthy sip. "You apologized by text that night and the next morning. And again when you called. But I'm not convinced you're truly sorry."

Rheo picked up a chip and threw it at her. Abi and Fletch shared the same dry sense of humor.

"It's all good, Rhee. Did you work it out with Fletch?"

"Yeah."

"And you now know there was just a glitch with his card?"

"I do." She wouldn't tell Abi she'd been given a peek at his bank account. "If I hadn't been so triggered, I would've remembered his top-of-the-line running shoes, all his tech toys, and the fancy watch. I've seen it. It can do everything but launch him to the moon."

Rheo put her bare feet onto the railing and used her wineglass to gesture to the busy street. "Have you never thought about opening during the evenings? You'd do well."

Abi took a fat black olive from the bowl on the wrought iron table between them. "*Ugh*, no. I'm too much of a control freak and I'd never take any time off. I'd be there 24/7. Nope, I'm happy doing what I'm doing."

Lucky girl. Rheo dipped a chip into homemade guacamole. Abi was so comfortable in her skin, so confident about her place in the world. Rheo thought she'd been the same when she was in New York, but in hindsight, she hadn't been, not really. Oh, she'd enjoyed her life and job, but she'd been constantly on edge, always looking around to see where she was, what could go wrong, looking for obstacles instead of seeking joy. She'd spent more time checking her plan and scanning the horizon for trouble than enjoying life.

"It's so nice to see you," Abi told her. "I've missed you lately."

Oh God, was she one of those awful women who vanished when a new man came on the scene? She slapped her hands on her cheeks, horrified. "Oh, have I neglected you?

God, I'm so sorry! And especially since you've been so good to me—"

Abi rolled her eyes. "Jeez, calm down. Trust me, if I had a hottie like Fletch in my bed, I wouldn't pay attention to my girlfriends either. I'm not pissed, Rheo. It's genuinely okay."

Uncertainty rippled through her. Could she believe that? Was Abi just being nice?

"I hated it when Carrie did that to me when we stayed here over the summer. We'd be getting along okay, then a boy would come along, and I wouldn't see her for the rest of the time. It happened once or twice in college too. I made a friend, she'd fall in love, and she'd disappear." And it hurt, dammit. Making friends became more hassle than it was worth, and she stopped, choosing to focus on her studies instead.

"I'm not a teenager, Rhee, and we're the type of friends who don't need to live in each other's pockets," Abi told her, sounding firm. She lifted her glass to her lips, her brown eyes full of mischief. "So, are you falling in love with Fletch, Rheo Whitlock?"

"Pfft. As if I would be *that* stupid!"

"What's stupid about falling in love?" Abi asked. "Love and finding your person is the lifelong goal of some people."

"I won't fall in love with Fletcher," Rheo clarified.

"He's smart, hot, financially fluid." Abi ticked off his attributes, and the last one made Rheo wince. Embarrassment still lingered.

"Adventurer, nomad, traveler, never in the country," Rheo retorted. "We're complete opposites. It would never work."

Abi shrugged. "I think anything can work, if people want it enough."

"Easier said than done," Rheo told her. "He and my cousin are very much alike, actually. Bold and bright and chasing the sun," she said, reaching for the wine bottle.

"Are they together?" Abi asked.

Not now. Of that much she was sure. "He said they are just friends, but you've seen Carrie's IG account. I'm pretty sure they must've hooked up at some point, because guys are never *just* friends with my beautiful cousin."

"She's one gorgeous *chica*," Abi agreed.

Right? "On paper, they are perfect for each other… They love the same things and enjoy the same life. And, God, they'd make *beautiful* babies."

"Yet the chemistry between you two is hot enough to power a town," Abi stated, grinning. "Every time you walk into my place, I feel the need to have the fire extinguisher close by."

Rheo grinned back. "It's the weirdest thing."

She rocked back in her chair, watching two women leaving a bar two doors along, smiling as they shared a kiss. Chemistry was one of life's great mysteries. Fletch walked into a room and her skin pebbled. He looked at her, and thoughts of what they did naked—dirty, lovely things—rolled over her and heated the space between her legs, causing her nipples to harden. Would the next man she dated make her feel like this? She doubted it. Fletch was a once-in-a-lifetime lover.

Abi lightly slapped Rheo's hand to pull her attention back.

"Get your mind out of the bedroom and drink your wine, Rheo."

Rheo blushed. After catching up on Abi's life and business, Rheo ran her finger around the rim of her glass. "Fletch wants me to step out of my comfort zone. He badgered me into taking a walk this morning."

"Where?"

"On the hiking trail above the Pink House."

Abi slapped her hands against her cheeks, pretending to be shocked. "Outside?" Rheo rolled her eyes. Abi grinned and dropped her hands. "And how was it?"

"Fun, actually. I mean, I'm never going to be a mountain climber, but it was nice," Rheo admitted. "We only walked for an hour. Fletch was very patient with me ambling along behind him."

"Tell me more about you getting out of your comfort zone?" Abi asked.

Rheo explained, and when she was done, Abi leaned back and crossed her legs. "I think he's right. I think you've let yourself get into a rut and haven't done anything to dig yourself out of it. I think if Fletch hadn't come along, your time would've run out and you would've been catapulted back into the real world, crashed, and maybe flamed out again."

She wanted to argue, but knew Abi was right. Before Fletch dropped into her world, she'd been hiding, unable to focus or make any decisions.

"He thinks I need to try other things I haven't attempted before. He believes my inability to translate is linked to my confidence. He's convinced that when I get my confidence back, I'll be able to work as well as I did before."

Abi nodded slowly. "I agree with him, Rheo. I think we should all push beyond our comfort zones. That's where the fun is, it's where we grow."

Yeah, but it was scary out there in the unknown. "He also thinks I should tell my family where I am and explain what happened at work."

"I've been telling you that for months!" Abi protested.

Yes, but it hadn't resonated until Fletch came along. She nodded to her phone, sitting on the table between them. "He suggested I call Carrie and tell her first. See how she reacts and then tell my parents."

"And Paddy?"

Rheo pulled a face. "Not ready to go there yet. I don't want to disappoint her, nor do I want to damage our relationship."

"Surely it won't come to that? Aren't you overreacting?"

It was a fair question, and one she'd considered. "Paddy is tricky," Rheo told her.

Last year, she couldn't see any fault in her grandmother, but she now recognized Paddy's assertiveness could be described as being bossy. Paddy didn't have, as the Spanish said—*sin pelos en la lengua*—any hair on her tongue. She was ridiculously direct and sometimes her straightforwardness tipped over into cruelty.

In some ways, Rheo's life, and the people in it, were a little like an old-fashioned photograph being soaked in a chemical solution, slowly gaining clarity with time.

"So, why haven't you phoned your cousin yet?" Abi asked.

"Because I'm a coward?" Rheo replied.

"Mmm-hmm." Abi snatched Rheo's phone off the table. Rheo scrambled out of her chair, and when she made it to Abi's side, her friend was inside the apartment and the video call was in progress. Right, she really needed to put a screen lock on her phone.

But Rheo wasn't too worried. Carrie wouldn't answer, she was far too busy—

"Who are you and why are you on Rheo's phone?" Carrie's familiar voice floated across to her.

"Hey, I'm Abi, Rheo's friend," Abi replied. She grabbed Rheo's arm and tugged her to her side. "Here's Rheo."

Carrie's smile was sweeter than she expected it to be. "Hi, Rhee," she said. "It's so good to see you."

Rheo smiled, thinking Carrie looked fantastic. Her cousin's face was makeup free, her long blond hair was beach-babe messy, and she wore a ratty, paint-splattered shirt. Rheo noted a smear of green on the side of her nose.

"Have you taken up painting again?" Rheo asked.

"I wish! No, paintball shooting."

Pity. Carrie was a talented painter. Rheo took the phone from Abi and they walked back onto the patio. When Abi turned to walk into the kitchen, wanting to give her some privacy, Rheo tugged her shirt and pulled her back. Abi sat down again, but Rheo leaned against the railing.

"Is that Gilmartin?" Carrie demanded, her eyes narrowing. "Are you in *Gilmartin*? What the hell, Rhee? You said you'd never go back there!"

Rheo gulped. "Well, that's why I'm calling you—"

"Where are you staying?" Carrie demanded, her voice rising. "Paddy rented the Pink House to a friend of mine, Fletch. Have you met him? Why aren't you telling me anything, Rheo?"

"Well, I would if you'd give me a minute to speak," Rheo told her, exasperated.

Carrie waved her hand and nodded. "Okay, *okay*!" Her silence lasted a second. "But how long have you been there and—"

"Carrie, shut up, okay?" Rheo shouted, feeling on edge. She moved to the closest chair and looked at Abi, who smiled in sympathy. "It's a long story, and I won't be able to tell you if you keep interrupting."

"Just tell me you are okay," she said, sounding anxious.

"I'm fine." Rheo never expected Carrie to be so worried about her. "Well, better than I was. I messed up at work, quite badly, and I went into a bit of a downward spiral," Rheo said, testing the waters. At the first hint of teasing from Carrie, she'd cut the call.

"What about Callum?"

"Ah, he dumped me before all this happened."

"The dick biscuit."

Abi half snorted, half laughed at Carrie's description. Carrie, to Rheo's surprise, just tipped her head to the side and waited for more. So far, so good.

"I was forced into a six-month sabbatical, and instead of staying in New York, I sublet my apartment and came here. I've been hiding out in Gilmartin for a while now."

Carrie's eyes got bigger and bigger, and Rheo, now on a roll, decided to tell her the rest. "I've been living in the Pink House, but Paddy doesn't know."

"But Fletch is living there," Carrie murmured, looking confused.

"His arrival was a bit of a shock. He agreed to let me stay, and I persuaded him to keep my presence in Gilmartin secret."

"But why?" Carrie wailed.

Here came the hard part. "Because I didn't want to tell any of you that my supposedly perfect life wasn't so perfect after all," she quietly admitted.

Carrie stared at her, her eyebrows lifting. "Honey," she drawled, "the only person who thinks your life is perfect is you. We think it's stressful and tough and very, very rigid."

Abi winced and Rheo felt two feet high. Right.

Carrie went on. "You're allowed to mess up, Rheo, for God's sake! So, your life didn't go to plan, it often doesn't!"

Carrie wasn't reacting the way Rheo expected her to, and that puzzled and annoyed her. They always dealt with each other in a certain way, had done so all their lives, but Carrie was reading from a new script. And Rheo didn't know her lines.

"So you and Fletch are staying in the Pink House together," Carrie mused, a small smile touching her face. "What do you think of him? He's cool, right?"

Of all the words Carrie could pick, "cool" was the last one Rheo anticipated. Hot, sexy, masculine… She'd braced herself to hear those. But Carrie's "cool" was friendly and held no sexual heat. Rheo frowned as she took in her wide smile. Was her idea of Fletch and her cousin hooking up in the past another of her stupid-ass assumptions?

So, what did she think about him? That he was the hottest, sexiest, nicest man she'd met? Ever? That he gave the best orgasms, and she loved talking to him more than any other person she could think of? That she was hovering on the edge of falling for him, conscious of losing her footing?

Rheo had no clue how to express her thoughts, so she just lifted one shoulder. "He's okay," she said.

Abi shook her head and rolled her eyes.

"Fletch and I have become..." she hesitated "...friends. He's encouraging me to come clean with the family."

"And he's right," Carrie snapped. "You keep yourself apart, Rheo, and pulling personal information out of you is like pulling blood from a stone."

Yes, well, that's what happened when you didn't fit in.

"So, are you going to tell your parents?" Carrie asked, gripping the bridge of her nose.

"At some point," Rheo replied.

"They'll be fine with it. They don't freak out when life does a three-sixty. Paddy, on the other hand, she's going to lose her shit when she hears your wonderful job is in jeopardy and that you've been living in her house without her permission."

"I know," Rheo said, sounding glum. "Please don't tell her, Carrie I need to. If she hears it from you, she'll be even madder at me."

Carrie nodded. "I'll keep it quiet, but the longer you

delay telling her, the angrier she'll be. Man, she's gonna be mad. You're her blue-eyed girl, literally. The one who got things right."

"And that's why I haven't told her yet," Rheo admitted. "I don't want to disappoint her."

"Oh, we've all disappointed her at some stage in our lives and the world keeps turning," Carrie told her, grinning. "Paddy's good opinion isn't the be-all end-all, Rhee."

No, it just felt like it.

"Even your dad has managed to keep going despite them not talking for a year," Carrie said, sounding sarcastic.

"Do you believe he asked to see Paddy's will?" Rheo asked.

Carrie looked surprised. "Are we still talking about this? Jesus, you and Paddy can't let things go! It happened so long ago—"

No, only twelve months…

"—but no, I don't. He said he didn't, and I believe him. Your dad doesn't mind being called a layabout or a drifter, but being called a liar caused more hurt than you or Paddy realize."

Great.

Somebody called Carrie's name and she turned around, bestowing her golden smile on someone off camera.

"I've got to go," she told Rheo. She lifted her finger and pointed it at Rheo, frowning. "Call Paddy and your folks. Oh, and I might be able to get to Gilmartin sooner than I thought. Do you want to do some climbing with Fletch and me?"

Rheo scowled at her mischievous smile. "I'm just going

to let my middle finger do the talking right now," she told her, with no heat in her voice.

Carrie laughed, disconnected, and Rheo tossed her phone on the table and looked at her friend. "Well, that went better than I thought."

"Good," Abi told her and pushed her glass of wine closer to her. "Now drink. I've never seen anyone who needs more of a buzz than you do right now."

Rheo reached for her glass, lifted it, and eyed the pale gold liquid. "Tequila would be better," she mused.

"Oh yeah." Abi grinned. "I've got you covered, girlfriend."

Because wasn't tequila like duct tape, able to fix anything?

The next morning, Rheo sat on the kitchen steps and prayed the little men digging trenches in her head would put down their tools and strike. Her stomach pitched and rolled, and she was lightheaded from too little food and way too much alcohol. What did she think she was doing tossing back tequila shots like there was no tomorrow?

Tomorrow had arrived and it was kicking her ass.

Ooh la, j'ai la gueule de bois. She'd never understood what having a wooden mouth felt like before today.

She nursed the cup of hot black coffee Fletch had pushed into her hands when she stumbled into the Pink House a half hour ago, having passed out around three at Abi's. Along with her pounding head, she was pretty sure sleeping on Abi's couch dislocated her spine and put her hip out of alignment.

Rheo pushed her hand through her hair and longed for bed. She wanted to crawl under the covers and sleep off her hangover, but Rheo believed part of being an adult was accepting the consequences of her actions. She might be on a sabbatical, but she couldn't sleep the day away.

Rheo looked across to where Fletch worked in the sunlight. He'd designed a new gazebo, bought additional supplies, and dug holes for the four posts. He was another reason she couldn't trundle up to bed. She'd promised to be his apprentice today, and he wasn't going to let her skulk away.

"Feeling a bit rough, Whitlock?" he asked, not bothering to hide his amusement.

Rheo stuck her tongue out at him. While Rheo looked—and possibly smelled—like a ratty dishrag, Fletch looked revoltingly healthy, energetic, and vital. He wore old jeans, a T-shirt, and a ballcap over his blond-brown hair.

"I hate you," Rheo informed him, resting her cheek on her knee.

"You know the old saying…one tequila, two tequila, three tequila, *floor*," Fletch told her, laughing. He poured water on a pile of concrete he'd heaped on an old piece of board, and, using a shovel, started to form a gray, lumpy paste.

"It wasn't one of my brighter ideas," Rheo admitted. She tapped her fingers against her mug. She stared down at her coffee, looking for her words. "So, I talked to Carrie last night."

Fletch lifted his eyebrows but didn't stop turning the concrete and water mixture.

"Good talk or bad talk?" he asked, not breaking his stride.

"It was better than I expected," Rheo admitted. She hadn't spoken to Carrie for any length for ages, yet her cousin had behaved as if they'd spoken only last week. There'd been no embarrassment or stilted conversation…not from Carrie anyway.

"Did you tell her you're hiding in Gilmartin, and you've taken a break from your job and life?"

"I did. She wasn't too fazed, to be honest."

"She wouldn't be. Carrie doesn't sweat the small stuff."

Rheo jerked, and her head rolled—*ow, ow ow!*—annoyed at Fletch calling jeopardizing her job and life *small*.

"She said she might be here sooner than she thought," Rheo said.

"Hmm, I know. She called me soon after she spoke to you," Fletch told her, dropping the spade and walking over to the pile of posts. He lifted one and pushed it to a standing position, and Rheo enjoyed the flex of his biceps. "I'm going to need your help here, Rhee."

She needed all her energy to remain sitting upright on the kitchen step, and he expected her to do manual work?

"I have a hangover, Fletch," she whined.

"Get your pretty ass over here, Whitlock."

It took Rheo ages to climb to her feet and walk the few yards to where he stood. She yawned as Fletch tipped the post into one of the four holes he'd dug and told her to hold it straight. When he turned away to shovel concrete into the hole, she allowed the post to rest on her shoulder. The sun on her head and face made her eyes flutter closed.

"Shit, Rhee, hold it straight," Fletch told her. He picked up a small, plastic thingamajig and placed it on the pole, staring at the bubble in the window of it and making minor changes to the pole.

"I'm using a spirit level to make sure the pole is straight." Okay…but she so didn't care.

"Keep the pole right there and do not let it move, at all," he ordered.

Wow, she rather liked this bossy side of him. But she preferred him to order her about in the bedroom. *Oooh, sex.* Sex would be fun. *Mmm.* Interesting that she was too hungover to live, but she still wanted sex. Maybe there was life beyond death…

"We can ditch this and go to bed," she told Fletch as he shoveled concrete into the hole around the base of the pole.

"After which you'll crash for the rest of the day." Fletch shook his head. "Nope, I want to get this done."

He'd refused sex to finish building a gazebo. What did that mean? She stared at his tanned neck and wondered if the bloom was off the rose, whether his excitement was fading. They'd been sleeping together for a month now and maybe boredom was setting in, his feet were getting itchy. God, she hoped not. She wasn't ready to say goodbye to him. Would she ever be?

"Carrie asked me what I thought about you," Fletch stated.

Oh… She pulled her bottom lip between her teeth before speaking. "And what did you tell her?" she asked, cursing when her tone wasn't nearly as casual as she wanted it to be.

"That you are a complete pain in my ass… You're not holding the pole straight, Rheo!" Fletch huffed, did his spirit-level thing again, and told her to hold it to the pole and to make sure the bubble didn't move. God, the *pressure*.

"Did you really tell her that?" Rheo demanded, increasing her grip on the pole and holding the spirit level to the wood, keeping her eye on the now straight bubble. "And more importantly, did you mean it?"

Fletch filled the hole with concrete, stood, and took the spirit level from her hands. "You can let go, Rheo, it'll stand on its own now."

She dropped her hands, expecting the pole to topple, but it stayed upright. Fletch walked to where she stood, took off his cap, and tugged it onto her head. "Your face is burning," he told her, dropping a kiss to the side of her mouth. "I also told her you are fun and lovely and asked why she hadn't introduced you to me sooner."

No way. Rheo stared at his broad back as he picked up a pole and moved it to another hole. He stood it upright, and Rheo handed him the spirit level without asking. His words soothed her battered spirit, and energy coursed through her veins, as she mentally danced. Mental dancing was all she was capable of.

Rheo helped Fletch as he moved from hole to hole, inserting the poles and tossing in concrete. His design was a lot more complicated, and lovelier, than hers, and would look stunning with a creeper covering it. She was grateful for his help and told him so.

"It's easy enough to build and I did knock yours down," he told her, smiling. "Admittedly, not hard to do."

She pulled a face at him before yawning.

"How was your evening?" Rheo asked. "What time did you get home?"

"At a very respectable ten thirty," Fletch replied. "Mick, Sam, and I played pool at Diego's."

He transferred concrete into the last hole before standing and resting his forearm on the handle of the spade. "Hey, have you heard about the Gilmartin Mud Race?"

She wrinkled her nose and frowned. "Should I have?"

"Probably not, since anything involving exercise is not your jam."

"I did enjoy our hike the other morning."

Fletch's smile was low, sweet, and slow. "*Walk*, not hike, but I'm glad. Anyway, the mud race is coming up soon and it's exactly as described—a muddy race but with obstacles. Mick and Sam want me to join their team and run it with them."

Rheo wondered at his lack of enthusiasm. Fletch loved running and a little mud wouldn't put him off. "You sound hesitant."

He pushed his hand through his sweaty hair. "I want to do it, but I don't think my doctor will approve of me doing a twelve-mile somewhat challenging obstacle run. I'm supposed to be taking a break from physical activity."

"You often run. You've rock-climbed and done a couple of long hikes," Rheo pointed out.

He shrugged off her words. "Yeah, but those weren't physically taxing at all."

So annoying.

"I refused to join the brothers on a forty-mile trail, but if I take part in this race, it'll get back to Seb and he will not be pleased. He's not only my doctor but my friend, and I don't like going behind his back." He pushed his hair off his face with his forearm. "The guys want to use the event and me joining their team as a way to promote their business."

"Don't you normally charge people to do that?"

He lifted his shoulder. "I like them. They work hard and are passionate about what they do. And, frankly, they couldn't afford to pay my fees. I don't mind helping them out. I just have to get the go-ahead from Seb first."

"Why is he monitoring your exercise?" Rheo asked, intrigued.

"My expeditions are grueling, and I tend to push myself too hard."

"Really?" Rheo asked dramatically.

"Haha, funny," he retorted. "Anyway, Seb tells the insurance company I'm healthy and fit enough to take on expeditions, and he's worried my body has taken a pounding lately, so he told me to cut back on pushing myself. Anyway, we're getting offtrack. I mentioned the mud race because I think it could help you."

No matter how hard she tried, she couldn't make the connection.

He placed a hand on her shoulder and squeezed. "I'm proud of you for calling Carrie, Rhee. You've taken the first step out of your comfort zone. It gets easier after this."

She adjusted the rim of his cap, squinting at him. Okay, she had a hangover, but she was battling to keep up with him this morning.

"I'm as worried about telling my parents now as I was before, and I'm still terrified of telling my grandmother."

"It'll be fine, Rheo. The anticipation is always worse than the reality," he said, running his hand over her shoulder. "Isn't living beyond the comfort zone fun?"

She glared at him. "No."

"If you wanted to do something different, something that would give you a massive confidence boost if you finished it, you could do the mud race."

She stared at him, convinced the hot sun had fried his brains. *Ich glaub mein Schwein pfeift?* Was her pig, as the Germans said, whistling?

"Me, do a twelve-mile mud race? Are you *batshit crazy*?"

"You could *never* do twelve miles," he said, dismissing the idea with a wave of his hand.

"I know! I wasn't the one who suggested it!" Rheo replied, nettled.

She needed to go inside the house, drink a pint of cold water to rehydrate, and swallow a handful of painkillers. And she also needed sleep.

"But you could do the fun race!" He wasn't budging off his shitty idea.

"I am *not* running, walking, or climbing over anything, especially if there's mud."

"You should. There's nothing quite like doing something outside your comfort zone and succeeding." He placed another pole in the last hole, and they made it straight, with Rheo holding it in place. "But you might need to join a team."

"I'm not a team player. Or a mud runner. Or a *runner*."

Did he not know her at all? There was zero fun in getting sweaty and breathless and dirty.

"I'll ask Mick and Sam to listen out for a team needing a fourth member," Fletch said, shoveling concrete into the last hole.

He wasn't listening, damn him. Hadn't heard a word. Rheo made sure the pole wouldn't topple before standing back. She turned to face Fletch, wound her fist in his shirt, whipped his cap off her head, and slapped it against his chest. "It's not happening, Wright! Not now, not anytime in the future. And, should I decide to live beyond my comfort zone, I'll choose what I want to do, not you."

"You'll change your mind," Fletch replied.

His patronizing smile set Rheo's teeth on edge. Because she was hungover, annoyed, edgy, and more than a little pissed off at his high-handed manner, Rheo placed her index finger on the pole and gently pushed. It didn't take much for the pole to lean, and when gravity started to work, it popped out of the concrete with a little *plop*.

Fletch cursed and Rheo walked off, thinking he could sort it out on his own. He believed he could manage her life, so he could manage this too.

She had a hangover to nurse and a midmorning nap to enjoy.

Eleven

Later that same day, her hangover gone, Rheo was now hungry, so she tossed chicken pieces in the air fryer. Her black bean, grilled chicken, and corn salad was one of the few meals she could prepare with any success. She took a bottle of water from the fridge, wondering where Fletch was. She hadn't seen him since their argument earlier, but she'd spent a lot of time thinking about his comments and her lack of interest in living outside her comfort zone.

Was she *such* an outlier? Was her reaction to Fletch's suggestion so out of the norm? Weren't most people interested in living steady, stable lives? The majority of the world wasn't like Fletch—someone who enjoyed living life on the edge of a hurricane.

He thrived on feeling out of his comfort zone. Most people didn't.

Most people didn't want to screw up, and everybody feared something...

Rheo sipped her water, and looked at majestic Mount Hood, pushing its way into the blue sky. She couldn't imagine climbing it, but Fletch conquered mountains double, nearly triple its height. He'd summited Everest, despite experiencing the avalanche the year before. The avalanche was the closest he had come to dying, and she absolutely understood his reluctance to go back to Nepal. Yet he'd done it. He faced his fear, looked it in the eye, and returned the following summer.

He'd kicked fear's ass.

Rheo tossed the chicken, still thinking. She wished she could be more like him, be someone who looked fear in the eye and stared it down.

He acknowledged it, but didn't let it affect his decisions. If he did, he would not have accomplished half the things he had, nor seen so many wild places. Did he find fear easier to handle because he'd been so sick as a teenager? Was the possibility of going back to physical weakness a far scarier prospect than falling off a mountain or walking into an impenetrable jungle with all its hidden dangers? To someone who took big bites out of life like Fletch did, she imagined it would be.

She'd looked up the mud race online and rolled her eyes at the "suitable for seniors and children under the age of twelve" description. Fletch believed completing the race would give her confidence, but Rheo didn't see how trying would make her look anything but stupid. She understood her strengths, and physical exercise wasn't one of them. She was uncoordinated and graceless, and the last time she ran, she'd prayed for a defibrillator and oxygen tank.

Plus, if she won—not a possibility—it would be winning

against old people and kids. Not a glorious achievement. If she finished near the back—highly possible—she would feel even worse. There was no upside to Fletch's suggestion…

She didn't want anything to do with the race. Rheo blew air into her cheeks. Compared to his extreme exploits, taking part in a mud race seemed so trivial. Yet, she categorically didn't want to. She didn't want to look foolish, to be forced to give up, to feel out of her depth.

She didn't want to feel out of control. She hated feeling like that. And she did not like to fail.

Failure, lack of control, and looking bad were some reasons why she'd yet to tell Paddy where she was and what happened. She feared Paddy's disappointment, just like Fletch had feared going back to Base Camp.

Shame washed over her. How could she compare her fear of disappointing Paddy to Fletch's avalanche? Her grandmother was a five-foot-two flesh-and-blood person, albeit one with a domineering streak. She wasn't a treacherous ice floe, a dangerous mountain, or a rock fall. Rheo had reached a new depth of ridiculousness.

And why was she waiting? There wouldn't ever be a good time to tell Paddy, and the situation would deteriorate the longer she left it. She needed to bite the bullet and get it done…

But before she told Paddy, she needed to tell her folks.

Carrie hadn't thought it such a big deal, and there was a fair chance her parents would have an equally laid-back attitude. As long as they didn't make any snide comments about karma, she'd be okay. Though, to be honest, it wasn't like she didn't deserve to be mocked a little. She'd been disgustingly arrogant and judgmental in the past. She wouldn't blame them if they couldn't resist a few jibes.

Rheo tossed the chicken again, drained a can of beans, and shucked the corn. When there was nothing left to do, she video-called her mom, hoping they were climbing a mountain or digging a well and couldn't answer. But luck wasn't on her side and her mom's face appeared on her phone. Rheo winced at her parched skin and deepening wrinkles. She routinely bought her mom expensive moisturizers, but she was pretty sure her mom never used them.

"Rheo, how lovely to see your beautiful face," her mom told her, placing her hand on her heart. "You're looking casual, darling. Are you having a day off?"

"Is Dad around, Mom?" Rheo asked.

Her mom yelled for her father, and Rheo winced, placing her free hand over her ear. Her dad popped his head around the van door, and when he saw her on the screen, his face split into a broad smile. Her father drove her nuts, but he loved her. He might like and understand Carrie better, but he *did* love Rheo.

And today, that was enough.

After catching up for a few minutes, Rheo turned her phone around so they could see her location. "I'm staying here, at the Pink House. I've been here for four—no, nearly five months."

They exchanged looks and neither seemed too surprised. "We thought something was wrong," Gail stated, sounding subdued. "We suspected you might've quit your job, but we didn't think you'd be in Gilmartin."

"Why did you think I lost my job?" she demanded.

"We saw the viral video of the UN hot-mic incident," her dad explained. "We immediately recognized your voice."

Oh crap. Her face flamed with humiliation. "You recognized *my* voice? Why didn't you say anything?"

Her father's expression turned sheepish. "At the time, we hadn't heard from you in a while. You weren't answering our calls. We went online to see what was happening at the UN, wanting, I guess, to connect with you. It popped up then. We assumed you'd tell us about it when you were ready."

The damn internet. Rheo rubbed her temple. "I'm sorry. I should've returned your calls."

"We presumed your grandmother was still complaining about that stupid will business and you took her side."

"You shouldn't have—" No, she wasn't going there; it wasn't her fight. It was Paddy and their issue. She no longer needed to be part of it. She stopped talking and gripped the bridge of her nose with her thumb and forefinger. "I didn't think you'd seen the viral video," she quietly said.

"Well, we did. And we thoroughly agreed with what you said!" Gail announced. "We are so proud of you for standing up for what you believe in!"

All good and well, but she should've switched her mic off and kept her mouth shut. If not for Nicole, she might've lost her job over the incident, as she told her parents.

"If you lose your job, something else will come along," Ed told her.

"I haven't lost my job," Rheo said, trying to hold on to her patience. "I've just been on a six-month sabbatical."

They both looked disappointed. "Ah, *pity*," her mom murmured.

Rheo straightened, all-too-familiar irritation shooting through her. "Adults need jobs, you know," she said. "I have to pay for my apartment and my food, build my savings. Help you guys out of a jam occasionally." Okay, the last jab was unnecessary, but their easy acceptance of her misfortune shocked her.

"We'd just prefer you to have more balance in your life," her dad said, his voice calm. "You don't seem to have much fun, darling."

She *had* fun. She *did*. She just couldn't think of an example right now.

Knowing she was on shaky ground, she changed the subject. "Anyway, I'm staying at the Pink House, but Paddy doesn't know."

Her dad rubbed his hands together, his eyes dancing with glee. "Excellent. Your news will take the heat off me."

Rheo rolled her eyes at her father. "Thanks for the support, Dad."

"Doesn't the Pink House have a tenant?" her mom asked.

"Mmm-hmm. We're sharing the place." Her parents didn't need to know she and Fletch were also sharing a bed. "Fletch is an old friend of Carrie's."

Her mom nodded. "She's spoken of him before."

Naturally. Fletch was an impressive guy. "So, have you

enjoyed your time away from the city, Rheo?" her dad asked, draping a hand around her mom's shoulder.

She started to say no, then hesitated. She was enjoying herself lately. Fletch's arrival made her world lighter and brighter. Apart from having a stunning sex life, they walked every day, and she'd come to enjoy being outside for a little while, sucking in the fresh air and the views, feeling her muscles stretching. They'd attended a few trivia and live music nights at Diego's bar, often ate at Abi's diner, and they'd spent many days on the lake, with her lying in the sun and paddling while Fletch SUP-ed or kayaked.

"It's been fine," she admitted. "Nice, actually."

"We're glad," her mom replied, and Rheo saw love in her eyes.

They might not be alike or understand each other, but she was *loved*. It wasn't their fault, nor was it hers, that they were so different.

"We would do anything for you, Rheo," her dad murmured. "If we could, we would."

She wished she'd had that reassurance when she was a child. Back then, she was always trying to catch up, running behind them while they strode on ahead, free and fearless.

She'd been the wrong child for them, they'd been the wrong parents for her...but it was okay. Maybe it was time to accept her childhood was over, time she moved on.

Rheo heard Fletch's Land Rover pull into its space next to the house. "Um...so, about Paddy. Please don't tell her I'm staying here?"

"I'm not talking to my mother, Rheo. Her choice, not mine," Ed said, his tone cold.

Rheo put her chin in her hand and looked at her dad. In his eyes, the same color as hers, she saw misery, defiance, and a lot of determination. Deciding to ask him the question she'd constantly avoided for the past year, she took a deep breath. "Dad, did you ask to see her will? Did you ask what you'd inherit?"

He didn't drop his eyes, nor did his eyes slide to the right or left. "Why would I do that?"

"Because you are worried about what you are going to do and where you are going to live when you get old? Because you wonder how you are going manage when you have to stop traveling because you are too old or sick?"

"No, I didn't ask to see her will. A friend of ours passed without one and it was a nightmare for his relatives, so I only asked if she had one."

Rheo believed him. He'd messed up a thousand times before in a thousand different ways, but this time, he spoke the truth.

He lifted his chin, obviously waiting for her criticism. He was expecting her to take a couple of potshots. What did it say about her that her father was expecting a lecture? Nothing good.

"I'm so sorry I didn't ask for your side of the story, Dad. That was wrong of me." She knew what he needed from her, so she gave him the only thing she could. "I believe you, Dad."

Ed closed his eyes, then he straightened, and Rheo caught the sheen of tears in his eyes. Knowing he needed a minute— her tough father didn't cry—she looked at her mom.

Gail cleared her throat. "Don't tie yourself in knots about

telling Paddy, Rheo. Your actions have no impact on her life," Gail said, sounding crisp.

"What do you mean?" Rheo asked, hearing Fletch opening the kitchen door. She smiled at him before turning her attention back to her mom. Whenever he walked into the room, his steady presence calmed her, it was as if her body knew that when he was around, all was well.

"You don't rely on her to pay your rent or your expenses, so she can't comment. It's your life, Rheo, not hers. Well, she shouldn't comment, but you know she will."

Rheo nodded. "I do."

Gail was right: it was her career, her life, and while she wasn't proud of letting everything fall apart, Paddy's life wasn't impacted by her failures.

Fletch held up a beer bottle for her, silently asking whether she wanted one. God, *yes*, this conversation required alcohol. She loved his thoughtfulness, and when this conversation was done, she'd step into his arms, lay her cheek on his chest and breathe in his scent. He was her emotional sanctuary and she ignored how the thought scared the shit out of her. She took the bottle, sipped, and lifted it in a silent toast to her parents.

"Now, as for you staying in Paddy's house without her permission," Gail told her, wincing, "I'm afraid you don't have a leg to stand on there. She's got a right to be annoyed about that."

The phone jiggled as Gail panned across the inside of the van, stopping on an ugly, dark brown pottery vase sitting on a high shelf, held in place with a bungee cord. "When she kills you, we'll put your ashes in a pretty vase and stash you next to Grandma Jean."

In a jar, on the road, with her parents. For eternity. *Awesome.*

The next day, Fletch was halfway out the door for a run when he heard the study door open. Pausing the fitness app on his phone, he stepped back into the hallway as Rheo walked out of the study.

Her face dropped as she took in his running gear. "Oh, you're going for a run," she said, sounding disappointed.

He waggled his eyebrows. "Make me a better offer and I'll gladly change my plans."

If she led him up to her bedroom—the room she'd allocated him to use the first day they met was now just a storage place for his stuff—it wouldn't be the first afternoon they'd spent in bed.

And every night, when she slid into bed beside him, warm, rosy, and lily-scented from her shower, he wanted her again. He couldn't imagine *not* wanting her.

A slightly terrifying thought for a Tuesday afternoon.

She wrinkled her nose in a way he found adorable. He also enjoyed her cloudy-with-sleep-eyes, her hum when she took her first sip of coffee in the morning, the way she always knew how far to take a conversation before it became too personal or awkward. The way she responded to him, with eagerness and trust...

She picked up her bare right foot and rubbed it behind her calf. "As much fun as that would be, do you think we could go for a walk? I need some fresh air."

They'd been walking regularly since he first dragged her out on the trail, but it pleased him that it was Rheo who made the suggestion. Seeing that she looked tired, and her frown suggested a headache, he resisted the urge to tease her, to check her forehead to see if she had a temperature because voluntarily asking to go for a walk wasn't something Rheo usually did.

"Sure, I'll walk with you."

It would mean giving up his run, but he was good with that. He could do some sit-ups and pull-ups later or do a quick HIIT workout. Being outside with her, ambling along at her slow-ass pace, was quickly becoming his second favorite Rheo-based activity.

Rheo flashed him one of those smiles that knocked the wind out of his sails. "Oh, and I just received a message from Carrie, saying she should be here next week sometime."

"I got the same message. I offered to collect her from the airport, but she said she already had a lift to Gilmartin."

"I hope she arrives before I leave. I haven't seen her for ages, and it would be good to catch up."

He was glad she and her cousin were talking again. He was not happy with the idea of her leaving. Rheo gestured to the stairs. "I'm just going to run up to change into my sneakers."

He sat on the bottom stair and exited his exercise app. Looking around the hall, he smiled at Paddy's photo. "I think I might be in trouble, Paddy."

He really liked Rheo. As in *like* liked. And God, didn't he sound like a teenager? Sure, these past few weeks spent with Rheo hadn't been adrenaline-fueled, but they'd still been exciting, in a low-key but equally thrilling way.

His body might've been resting, but his heart felt like it was consistently throwing itself off a cliff. The sex they shared was intense, their conversations intellectually challenging, their silences easy.

He'd always been wary of emotional closeness, but sharing space with her seemed as natural as breathing. He could no longer avoid the obvious…he was wading through the shallow waters of a fling into the deep waters of a relationship.

And that was unacceptable, impossible. Being in a relationship could hinder his freedom to explore the world. And let's not forget that if he didn't stay on the shore, in the inch-deep water, he'd experience the hurt and disappointment of losing someone he'd come to enjoy and rely on. And that would be seriously shitty.

Awa' an bile yer heid.

His nan's favorite saying popped into his head. He had no idea how telling someone to "boil their head" translated to overreacting or making a needless fuss. But the Scottish message resonated; he might be making too much of nothing.

He would just have to be sensible and try to stay in the shallows.

A few days later, in Portland, Fletch rolled off Seb's examination table, walked over to the visitor's chair, and dropped into the seat, stretching out his long legs. He watched Seb write in his file, his handwriting an indecipherable scrawl.

Fletch had driven into Portland earlier, stopping to check on his tiny house before meeting up with Seb. In the small space, he'd felt hemmed in, so he flung the back door open and sat on the step, enjoying the early-morning sun on his face.

This was the first time he'd been properly alone in weeks. Oh, he and Rheo weren't joined at the hip, but he always knew where she was, whether that was in her study gabbling away in Spanish, French, or Italian, visiting with Abi or in the garden tugging up Paddy's flowers.

Conversation with Rheo came easily, their silences were never awkward, and she knew more about him, and his past, than ninety-nine percent of the people in his life. They'd been living together in the Pink House for over a month now, and he'd yet to feel the urge to pack up and move on. He was still waiting for the familiar feelings of irritation and being cooped up to arrive.

Was it possible his stone had stopped rolling? God, what a thought.

Seb looked up, closed the file, and leaned back in his chair. "Your checkup is over, you can breathe."

"Everything good?' Fletch asked, loathing his need for reassurance.

"Your bloodwork is fine."

That was good to hear. Fletcher leaned forward. "So, I want to do a twelve-mile obstacle course in a couple of weeks. I was just going to do it without telling you, but I thought you deserved better."

Seb sat back, folded his hands on top of the file, and nodded. "I do."

"So, do I have your permission to do the run?"

"Even if I gave it, you would do whatever you wanted to," Seb said, an annoying smirk on his face.

Strangling the dude was an option. Fletch scowled at him, thinking his comment didn't deserve a response.

Seb tapped his file with his index finger, taking his time. "We've always operated on a 'see how your body feels' basis, Fletch. You know how you feel. Do you feel fit enough to do this race?"

He did. He wasn't at his fittest, and he would need to do some serious training before he undertook another expedition, but he was relaxed, healthy, and energetic. "I do. It won't be hard, and it's not something I'm feeling competitive about or taking that seriously."

Yeah, he was self-reliant and independent, but Seb was one of the few people whose advice he'd listen to. He was slowly learning to open up and lean on other people, just a little.

"CFS is a tiny bastard that sits on my shoulder, taunting me about coming back. It's my biggest fear."

Seb's eyes didn't leave his. "I can't promise you that it will never return, but I can say you've been through a lot—pneumonia, malaria, frostbite, that damned scorpion sting in Zimbabwe. None of those triggered its return, but it's only been four weeks, and I'd like you to take it easy for a while longer, at least another month if you won't take the full three I recommended."

"I am fine, Seb. I'm not expedition fit, but a twelve-mile run won't cause me any issues."

"Unlike the forty-mile trail run you passed on a few weeks back," Seb murmured.

He knew he'd hear about it.

Seb lifted one shoulder. "You've picked up the weight you lost, and your vitamin levels are back to normal. Look, I have no medical grounds for asking you to delay the resumption of your training schedule. You're well rested, and you look a lot brighter than you did the last time I saw you. Do the race, Fletch, if that's what you want to do. I'd still like you to take it easy for another month, to only exercise enough to keep up your fitness levels, and to take more than your usual rest days."

Fletch thought his suggestion more than fair. He needed time out to get his head straight, to give his body more time to recover. "You were right," he told Seb, who grinned. "Don't get used to hearing that."

"So, what's the plan? Do you still want to visit the Danakil Depression?"

He didn't know how to answer that.

He now had Rheo in his life, and that was more heat than he could currently handle. He had decisions to make, one of which was how to reconcile his desire for freedom and his growing feelings for a woman who craved stability.

Chasing the horizon was something he knew how to do. The world was vast, and he still wanted to see every corner of it and experience everything it had to offer. But now there was Rheo...

Shit, what was he supposed to do about her?

It was far easier to think and talk about his career.

"I'm not sure what to do," he told Seb after explaining the offer he'd received to do the shorter but still brutal scientific expeditions. "It's three to four months in very inhospitable places. Or I could give it a miss and go back to doing long-ass expeditions, sticking to my brand."

Seb played with his pen. "If not Danakil, do you have something in mind?"

"Maybe something along the lines of conquering the ten highest mountains, putting a deadline on it so that we race the clock?" Fletch tried to ignore the lack of enthusiasm in his voice. "Or we could explore North Africa, cross some deserts."

Seb grimaced. "I'm not a fan of dust and heat."

Neither was he, to be fair. But you couldn't avoid the places you didn't like if you wanted to explore every inch of the planet.

"Nims Parja climbed the fourteen highest peaks in six months, so your expedition might be anticlimactic."

"Nims is unbelievable. Part machine, part mountain goat," Fletch replied. "He's a specialist climber. I'm not."

"I'm voting for the Lazarus expeditions. It might be interesting to do something different, and I know the crew would enjoy shorter stints away."

"Mmm-hmm, Gavin told me told me his new wife wants him home more often than not." Fletch didn't want to lose Gavin—he was a great cameraman and one of the few who could keep up with him.

"Damned wives," Seb said, smiling. "How rude to expect their husbands to spend time at home. Luckily, I'm divorced and the rest of us are single."

Fletch thought about Rheo, hating the thought of spending the best part of a year away from her. Sure, he had a sat phone and could occasionally video-call, but not being able to hold her, see her smile, hear her laughter—make love to her—for months on end wasn't something he wanted to contemplate.

Dammit, how and why had his brief affair turned into something more, something deeper, and...well, *necessary*?

He couldn't, for one minute, imagine giving up his work—it meant everything to him—but he didn't want to be apart from Rheo for long stretches either.

He wanted to come home to Rheo.

Shit, this wasn't part of the plan...

Seb's office manager popped her head around the door and asked Seb if he could take a call, and Fletch waved him on. He needed a couple of minutes alone to get his wayward thoughts under control. What the hell was he thinking?

Was he thinking?

Seb's call was short, and within a few minutes he was back. "Where were we? Oh, talking about relationships."

Yeah...

"Our careers are hell on the people we love, aren't they?" Fletch quietly asked, leaning forward and linking his hands between his legs.

Seb had gotten divorced eight years ago, partly because he spent months in the jungle or on ice with Fletch, partly because his wife couldn't cope with the loneliness and cheated on him with his best friend.

Seb nodded, his expression somber. "We've watched more than a few relationships fall apart because of what we do, who we are. We can't be at home, they can't cope with us not being home, and it all gets messy."

Fletch hated being confined more than most. His crew didn't have the same issues around staying in one place as he did. They loved the freedom, loved the challenges, loved what they did, but his need not to be confined was more of a compulsion than a desire to see what was around the next corner.

He had to be able to leave, and what woman would tolerate him routinely walking out the door? It was why he avoided relationships, why he skimmed through life, not allowing his emotions to attend the party.

And wasn't it funny that the one woman who'd tempted him was the last woman he should have fallen for, someone who craved stability more than Buddhist monks craved enlightenment? He and Rheo were so different, poles apart in every way. He loved the outdoors, and while she didn't hate it anymore, she wasn't ever going to be a *"let's go hiking and camping"* type. She craved stability and security; he thought they were vastly overrated. She was into languages and literature; he read biographies and books on travel expeditions. He needed to see what he could find around the next corner. She didn't.

But she made him laugh and she made him think. And God, she made him burn. Rheo could walk into a room and a million tiny fireworks exploded in his stomach, while at the same time, his heart sighed and settled, at ease and happy. She was the person he most wanted to spend time with…

But it would never work, not in the long term.

If they wanted more than this step out of time, this hot affair, then one of them would have to make enormous compromises for them to be together. He would have to try and fit into her nine-to-five world, and it would kill him. Or she could give up a job she loved and travel with him to far-flung places, hanging around in strange towns, waiting for him to walk off a mountain or out of a jungle. That wasn't Rheo. She liked her job. She liked having a base, a home.

He didn't think they could work. How would they build a life, have a family, or grow old together? Resentment would eventually kill any love and affection. He wasn't in love with Rheo—he was damn close, but he refused to fall. Why take the path that ended in pain? He didn't want to experience the anguish of heartbreak, but he especially didn't want Rheo to be miserable. She'd experienced enough emotional agony at the hands of her family.

No, it would be better to put some distance between them, to cool things down. He wanted to be a great memory—he didn't want to be a source of pain. Besides, she practically had one foot out the door anyway. In ten days, she'd return to Brooklyn.

It made sense for him to spend a few more days in Portland, on his own, and when he returned to Gilmartin, Carrie would be there. He and Carrie would go on some overnight hikes, do the Little White Salmon run, and spend time out of the house. He could, by degrees, ease out of Rheo's life, and hopefully, disengaging wouldn't hurt too much.

He was bullshitting himself. Of course it would hurt, but as long as Rheo remained unscathed, he'd cope. Maybe. Hopefully.

Seb coughed and Fletch lifted his head. "You've met someone, haven't you, Fletch?"

What was the point of denying it? "Yeah."

"Fuck." Seb released a long sigh.

"It's a complication and I need to pull back." Fletch raked his hand through his hair. "I'm going to distance myself before we get hurt. When I get back to Gilmartin, I'll sign up for some hikes, some soloing and kayaking, things to get me out of the house. She's not into any of that shit."

Seb placed his hands behind him. "Do you want some company?"

God, *yes*. Fletch gestured to his messy desk. "Can you take time away?"

Seb worked as a specialist expedition doctor and only worked with individuals who put their bodies under extreme duress. He didn't have a heavy book of appointments, but when he did consult, he charged a fortune. "I can take a couple of weeks. I'll have to find somewhere to stay."

"Stay at the Pink House," Fletch told him. "I'm renting it and there are lots of bedrooms."

"Excellent," Seb replied.

As they made additional plans, doubt rolled over Fletch, cold and relentless. It was the right thing to do—there wasn't a hope for him and Rheo working long-term. He was trying to protect her, protect himself.

It was the right thing to do.

Wasn't it?

But it wasn't like he had a long list of choices. Or any at all.

Twelve

The sound of a growly engine pierced the silence of the afternoon and Rheo flew to the study's bay window. Fletch was back! Kneeling on the seat, she felt her heart sink as she watched an F-150 trundle past the Pink House and turn left at the T-junction.

Rheo sat on the window seat and stared at the hardwood floor, cursing her burning eyes. Where was Fletch? She'd thought he would be in and out of Portland, but this was day four and he was ignoring her messages. They'd never really defined their relationship, discussed what they were becoming to each other, but didn't she deserve just one "not sure of my plans, will be back when it suits" message?

Damn it! She would not slide back into that mental morass of second-guessing and overanalyzing herself. She was better than this! She wasn't someone who stressed about where her lover was, who spent hours thinking about what he was doing.

Or, God, *who* he was doing.

On those all too rare occasions when Callum told her he couldn't see her because of work pressures, she'd relished the freedom of uninterrupted time. She'd enjoyed her first Fletch-free day but missed him that night. Then missing turned to longing, and doubts and insecurity steamrolled her.

What was he doing in Portland? Was he sleeping with someone else? They hadn't made any promises to be exclusive.

But the truth was, part of her *wanted* to be exclusive.

She was in love with the man.

The realization hit her the second night she spent alone in her bed. She wanted to sleep with Fletch for the rest of her life.

He was the only person she would make sacrifices for. She didn't have a clue how to reconcile their vastly different lives, didn't have the faintest idea where to start or what a life spent together would look like, but she knew she wanted to try.

Her happiness simply lay with Fletch.

But judging by his lack of contact, his future didn't include her. And, God, it hurt more than anything else she'd felt since losing everything.

A rattling, vaguely familiar sound drifted through the open window, and Rheo looked down. A battered van braked in front of the house, announcing its arrival with a high-pitched squeal. She hadn't seen the van for over ten years, but it looked exactly the same, a faded powder blue as familiar as her signature. They hadn't fixed the ding above the tire, nor the long scratch on the driver's door.

Jesus Christ, her parents were here.

What the crap were they doing here?

Rheo ran into the hall and skidded on the smooth floor.
She yanked open the front door and flew down the steps,
cursing when one of Paddy's iceberg rosebushes snagged
her shirt. She wrenched it free and passed through the gate
leading to the sidewalk, reaching the van as her dad stepped
out. She braked, not sure how to greet him. They'd never
been touchy-feely types. Her dad took that decision out of
her hands, pulling her into a brief, hard hug. Gulping, Rheo
turned to kiss her mom's cheek, inhaling her wild sage perfume. Rheo lowered her head and noticed the familiar rings
on her mom's big and baby toes, the intricate tattoo covering the top of her right foot.

Her parents were here…

Yes, they infuriated her, she didn't understand them, but
it was still good to see them.

"And me? Don't I get a hug?"

Rheo's eyes widened as her cousin stepped onto the pave-
ment, a vision of tanned skin, blond hair, and bright green
eyes in a happy face.

The gang was all here…

Right. Well…

Okay then.

Carrying her cousin's backpack, Rheo followed Carrie
to the room she always used, the smaller one at the back
of the house. Rheo threw her pack onto the bed, still covered by a quilt that Grandma Jean, her mom's mom, made
for Carrie's tenth birthday. Rheo had been gifted one too,
but hers was in storage back in Brooklyn. Because she'd put
the quilt into a plastic bag and kept it away from sunlight, it

was brighter than Carrie's. But her cousin's seemed warmer, lovelier somehow, despite its faded squares. More interesting.

It was an apt metaphor for their lives. Hers was shiny and bright, but Carrie's was *way* more interesting.

Carrie flopped backward onto her bed, and Rheo perched on the edge of a wingback chair, confused. "Okay, explain again…why are you all here?" she demanded.

Carrie leaned back on her elbows and shook her head to move her hair off her face. "Your parents drove here from Houston—"

"Texas?"

"Houston, British Columbia," Carrie corrected her. "They came because they sensed a thaw in your attitude, and they wanted to capitalize on it. It's also a good time for them to return to Gilmartin, because Paddy is halfway across the world."

Rheo ran her fingers across her forehead, trying to take it all in.

"I'm here because I told Fletch I would be. Your parents said they'd pick me up if I flew into Seattle, so I did. I hope we can spend some quality time together…if you can yank the stick out of your ass."

Rheo frowned at her. "What stick?"

"The I'm-so-better-than-you-I've-got-life-sorted stick," Carrie told her.

Rheo wanted to retaliate, but her hot words died in her throat. She bit her lip, forcing herself to admit that she could sound prissy and pretentious. She echoed Paddy, and took her cues from her grandmother, never stopping to consider her family's feelings. That ended, today. Right now.

"I'm not better than you, and I don't have my life sorted," Rheo murmured.

Carrie flashed her megawatt smile. "Good girl. Where is Fletch?" she demanded, sitting up to tackle the buckle on her sandals.

"Currently, he's in Portland," Rheo told her, blinking at the change of subject.

"When is he back?"

"I have no idea," she answered, unable to keep the frost out of her voice. Had he forgotten how to use the damn phone? Were his fingers broken?

"Ooh, you look pissed off." Carrie tossed a sandal in the general direction of the cupboard. "What has he done?"

Rheo might as well share—she wouldn't be able to keep their affair secret now that the Pink House was full of her family. Nor did she want to. She wanted Carrie to know she and Fletch were together...that Fletch was attracted to her.

Ego again, Whitlock? When are you going to stop feeling second best?

"We're sleeping together."

Carrie's green eyes narrowed in concern. For her or for Fletch? Probably for Fletch. They were far closer than Rheo and Carrie were.

"He went to Portland, and I have no idea when he's coming back. He hasn't called or texted," Rheo added, shoving her hands into her hair. "I thought there was..." Her words trailed away, and she lifted her shoulders to her ears. Was she reading too much into this? Creating something out of nothing? They'd never agreed on a relationship...

"Oh, God, Rhee, I hope you're not falling for him," Carrie

said, sounding appalled. "He's an awesome guy, one of my best friends, but he's the *definition* of unavailable. He's emotionally distant and solitary. And his work—work that takes him away from civilization for the best part of the year—is his life."

She wasn't telling Rheo anything new. And still the words felt like a punch to her head and a kick to her kidneys.

Carrie scooted forward and laid her hand on Rheo's clenched fist. Carrie waited for Rheo's eyes to meet hers. "He's not your type, Rhee, you are not *his*. And, no, I'm not jealous, nor do I want him myself. I'm saying it because he's a good friend and you're my cousin, and I know you both. You are oil and water, ice and heat…you don't *work* together."

Rheo pulled her top lip between her teeth and furiously blinked, trying to dispel the tears threatening to fall.

"I'm not trying to be a bitch," Carrie quietly assured her. "I'm *really* not, Rhee. I just don't want you to get hurt. We might not be close, and this might be the first time we've spoken in ages, but you are part of the fabric of my life."

Rheo managed a small smile at Carrie's earnest face. Her cousin still called a situation exactly how it was and, of the two of them, she knew Fletch best.

He wasn't into Rheo emotionally…

Shit.

Needing to be alone, Rheo stood and handed Carrie a watery smile. "It's good to see you, Carrie."

And it was. As she'd said, Carrie was part of the fabric of her life, a brightly colored patchwork square.

"Be honest, you'd far prefer me to stay away so you wouldn't have to face the truth."

Rheo shook her head. "No, my days of shoving my head

in the sand are over." She folded her arms and rocked on her heels. "I need to think about my return to work, and I have to tackle Paddy."

Carrie grimaced. "Better you than me."

"Mmm-hmm." Rheo gestured to the door. "I should go see if the parents have settled in."

"Don't bother," Carrie told her, lifting her suitcase onto the bed. "They told me they want to sleep in the van, and they'll use the downstairs bathroom."

"How long are they staying?" Rheo asked. While she and her parents had declared a truce, she knew the three of them got along far better when many, many miles separated them. International borders were good, and continents between them better.

Carrie grinned. "Dunno! But it could always be worse…"

Rheo lifted her eyebrows. "How?"

"Paddy could fly in from Oz."

"*¡Estoy de un humor que mejor ni te cuento!*"

"Translation?" Carrie asked.

Rheo shrugged. "I'm in a mood, not happy…something like that."

"Ah, so…situation normal then?"

On the way out the door, Rheo picked up her cousin's sandal and lobbed it in the general direction of Carrie's head. When Carrie's laughter followed her onto the landing, she cursed her inability to hit anything more than three feet away.

Fletch's lips curved into a smile when he saw Carrie's incoming video call. "Hey, you! Where are you—"

Instead of smiling at him, Carrie's arched eyebrows pulled

together in a fierce frown. "I'm in Gilmartin, jerk head, and you aren't here!"

Sitting in a busy coffee shop with Seb, Fletch winced. "Why didn't you tell me? I would've made sure I was back by the time you arrived."

Fletch half turned his phone to show Seb Carrie's face, and Seb rolled his eyes. His best friend wasn't one of Carrie's fans. He had no idea why.

"Why haven't you told Rheo where you are and when you will be back?" Carrie demanded, with her usual in-your-face verve.

That was his business, and he didn't answer to Carrie, as he informed her. He took her off the video call and put the phone to his ear to ensure their conversation stayed private.

"Oh, bullshit, Fletch! She's my cousin. She's not a woman you can pick up and discard at the drop of a hat. You've spent the last six weeks with her. She's entitled to a little courtesy from you."

Her words held enough truth that shame, close to the surface whenever he thought about Rheo, swamped him. Carrie was right. Not contacting Rheo and ignoring her was a dick move. But Carrie didn't understand that Rheo was very different from anyone he'd met before. He couldn't just take little bites out of her, he wanted to gulp and devour. He wanted *everything*.

But everything was impossible.

"Well?" Carrie demanded.

"I'm not discussing my relationship with Rheo with you, Carrie," Fletch told her, lowering his voice. If he couldn't talk to Rheo, then he had no right discussing her with Carrie.

"Fair enough," Carrie conceded. "But can I tell you something about my cousin, Fletch?"

He didn't need any insights from Carrie. He'd messed up; he didn't need her sticking her nose in. Carrie, being bold and pushy, didn't wait for an answer to her question.

"She's got this huge brain, Fletch, but she's sensitive, far more than you'd believe. She thinks she's a hard-ass like Paddy, but she's not. She's so much nicer than our grandmother. When Rheo gives someone her time and attention, she becomes emotionally invested."

"We never—" Fletch said, stopping abruptly.

"Yeah, maybe she thought she could handle a fuck buddy situation. But she can't. Her feelings get involved. She would never have slept with you unless she felt something!"

And how was he supposed to know that? And why was this his fault?

Carrie answered his questions. "She's lonely, Fletch. She might not accept that, might not even know she is, but she's always been lonely, from the time she was little. She thinks she doesn't need people, but she *does*. Unfortunately, she's always chosen romantic relationships she can easily walk away from, men who don't touch her emotionally."

Fletch frowned, caught in an emotional squall. "What do you want me to do, Carrie? What can I do?"

She might not recognize it, but his was a genuine appeal for help. He couldn't have a relationship with Rheo, but he didn't want to let her go. He definitely didn't want to hurt her. Not sure which way to jump, he'd left Gilmartin, hoping the problem would resolve itself.

Another dick move.

"If you don't see this going anywhere, *tell* her. If you think it can, *tell* her. Do not ignore her texts, dick biscuit."

He winced. Carrie disconnected and Fletch lowered his phone, staring at the blank screen. He now had two Whitlock women pissed off with him. *Excellent.*

He met Seb's eyes and grimaced.

"Maybe I shouldn't come to Gilmartin with you," Seb said, rubbing the back of his neck.

Seb was as allergic to emotional scenes as Fletch was, but he wasn't going to let his friend back out now. "You *are* coming to Gilmartin with me, and we are going to hike and climb and spend time on the lake. Or does being around Carrie scare you that much?"

Seb shocked him by nodding. "She does," he replied.

And Fletch, knowing how tough Seb was, wondered what the hell Carrie had done to him.

Abi placed the steaming casserole on the kitchen table and dropped a kiss on Rheo's head. "I'm going to leave you now. You guys need to catch up."

Rheo spun around in her seat and sent her a *don't leave me* look. Abi had saved her life today when Rheo sent her a frantic text, informing her that her parents had arrived and that her fridge and pantry were empty. Abi arrived with dinner, bags of produce, and enough wine to float a battleship. Or, at the very least, a small canoe.

"Join us, Abs," Rheo implored. With Abi there, she wouldn't feel left out when their conversation turned to whether Yosemite was better than Yellowstone, or Huntington Beach was a better surf spot than Cocoa Beach.

Her parents and Carrie chimed in, asking her to stay. Abi wrinkled her nose and shook her head. "I'll join you another time."

Rheo walked Abi to her car and, in the driveway, hugged her again. "Thank you so much, Abs. I'm so grateful to have you in my life."

Abi squeezed her hand. "You look shattered, Rhee."

Rheo pushed her hand into her hair and dragged it away from her face. "I am. It's been a day. I expected Carrie to arrive at some point, but I never expected my parents to visit."

Abi swung her car key around her index finger. "Still nothing from Fletch?" she gently asked.

Rheo pursed her lips. "No."

Abi grimaced. "Ouch." She frowned and snapped her fist around her keys. "He hasn't taken his stuff, has he?"

No, she'd checked.

"Well, maybe there's a good explanation for why he hasn't contacted you."

"And maybe it's his way of reminding me I have no claim on his time, nor do I have a right to know where he is or what his movements are," Rheo snapped.

"Or that," Abi agreed.

Damn, not the response she'd hoped for.

She wanted Abi to tell her he'd lost her number or he was busy or give her a stupid-ass excuse for him not calling. But because Abi was brutally honest, she gave it to Rheo straight. Fletch, the asshole, was avoiding her.

Returning to the house, Rheo slipped into her chair opposite her dad and, despite not being hungry, spooned food onto her plate. She hadn't eaten today. Food, even Abi's, held no interest for her.

Rheo pushed her food around, half listening to Carrie recounting her hike up an active Balinese volcano and her parents discussing the death of a rock climber in Yosemite.

"Well, if you climb without ropes, what the hell can you expect?" Rheo snapped, after listening to their mournful comments about how sad it was and how only the good die young.

Her mom broke the uncomfortable silence. "He didn't die soloing. He died from double pneumonia after a bout of flu."

"Oh."

Right, she'd grabbed the wrong end of *that* stick. Rheo placed her elbow on the table and rubbed her forehead with her fingertips. She was emotionally and physically wiped out. She wanted to go to bed, but knew she would spend another night watching the shadows on the ceiling. She couldn't concentrate enough to read, and her mind tumbled from Fletch to work and back to Fletch.

Neither subject was easy to think through. Was she ready to go back to the UN? And if she wasn't, what else could she do? Would she ever sleep with Fletch again? Even *see* him again? No, that was silly—she'd speak to him soon, but it was doubtful they'd go back to what they were before. Whatever that had been.

She hated this, hated not knowing where she stood. This was why she should've kept her emotional distance and stayed uninvolved. The sex they shared was great, amazing, but was it worth all these *What's happening?* and *I'm so confused* thoughts?

Gail's hand on her arm pulled Rheo's attention back to the

table and her uneaten food. "So, tell us everything that happened, Rhee. I suspect you left lots out when we last spoke."

Yeah, she did. Because she didn't want them to know about her fall from grace. But should it matter? These people gave her life. She could keep her pride, or she could take some steps toward having a closer, more truthful relationship with them. Her pride and ego wanted to keep her mistakes under wraps—she didn't want to admit to failing. But wasn't failing how one learned? And she was so tired of trying to get it all right. Frankly, chasing perfection was exhausting.

Rheo pushed her plate away, skimming over her and Callum's breakup—it didn't hurt, they were still friends—and the events before and after the viral video. All three looked horrified when she told them severe stress led to her losing her words.

"I've lost my confidence, and I need it to do my job," Rheo admitted. "I've done a lot of training videos, but I will only know whether I can handle it when I'm in a high-pressure situation."

"But you're better than you were?" Carrie asked, topping off their wine.

Rheo considered her question. "Much. Something clicked when I translated for the Brazilian kayakers—long story—and from then, it hasn't been so hard. But I don't know, can't decide, whether I'm at the same standard I was before."

Ed rested his forearms on the table, his sandy, bushy eyebrows pulling together. "Is going back to that high-pressure environment something you want to do?"

"Are you telling me I should do something less stressful?" Rheo demanded, on the defensive. "Is it too *corporate* for you, Dad? Should I buy a van and hit the road?"

"No, I don't want you to do what we do, you'd hate it."

She'd forgotten how literal her father was. He didn't do sarcasm.

"You always hated it. But you don't have to return to a job you don't want to do either," Ed continued, his eyes holding more patience than she deserved.

Rheo's temper subsided as quickly as it rose. "Sorry, Dad, it's a hot button."

"I know," Ed replied. "Our hot button is you criticizing our lifestyle. It's not fun knowing your only child thinks you are moronic for doing what you do, for the life you live."

Oh... *Bullseye, Dad*...straight to the heart. Rheo faced a choice. She could change the subject, or they could pull their issues into the light and deal with them.

"It's no secret that I hate that you can't support yourselves without taking the occasional handout," she said, choosing her words carefully.

Rheo heard Carrie's gasp, but she kept her eyes on her father's face. "I hate it when you take money from people—" she swallowed "—from *me*, and promise to repay it and then don't. That you sweep it under the carpet and hope I forget about it. I don't forget, and every time you break your word, another piece of me cracks."

When had she last been this honest? Rheo couldn't remember. But it was time to open the wound and inspect it, as ugly as it was. Maybe if they could flush it out, they could find a better way to deal with each other in the future.

"We've had bad luck," Gail protested. "Not everything was our fault!"

No, she wasn't going to let her mom play the victim. "You

made choices, Mom! In every way and every day, you made choices. Both of you got good job offers! I was there, I heard you talking about them. But something always went wrong. You got bored, or a boss was mean to you! Or someone was going somewhere, and you wanted to tag along!"

Hearing her voice rising, Carrie touched her arm. "Easy, Rhee."

Rheo nodded. Her eyes connected with Gail's, and she lifted one shoulder. "You can't keep blaming circumstances, Mom. You chose this life, you chose it over *me*. Every decision you made had consequences attached to it."

Gail ran her thumbnail along the edge of her plate. "Do you think we should've settled down when you came along?"

Should they have put her happiness above theirs? Should two people be miserable instead of one? She didn't know. How much were parents supposed to sacrifice for their children? Everything? Nothing? Something in between?

"I don't know. I can't answer that. I'm just glad I came off the road when I did."

"We lost you to your grandmother," Ed stated bitterly, after throwing back his wine. "Once she got her claws into you, we didn't have a chance in hell."

Paddy had never made any bones about how much she despised her son's lack of ambition, Ed's complete inability to conform, and Rheo's parents' quest for freedom.

"Paddy's love of structure and organization appealed to me," Rheo carefully replied. And, yes, because she adored her grandmother, because she'd given Rheo a sense of stability when she'd most needed it, she had modeled her life after Paddy's and taken on her opinions. Paddy's life made sense to Rheo… But, along with her ambition and drive, she'd also absorbed Paddy's judgmental streak.

Paddy liked things the way she liked them and so did Rheo. But their way didn't suit everybody. Being confined to an office life would've killed her father. Or worse, it would've killed his delight in the world and his adventurous spirit. He and Fletch were alike in that way. Was that why Fletch was ignoring her? Because he'd stayed in the same place for too long and was feeling jailed?

She couldn't think about Fletch now; she needed to concentrate on her parents.

"What happens when you get too old to be on the road? You don't have a house, medical insurance, or a consistent source of income. What happens then?"

Ed cleared his throat and his normally quick-to-smile mouth tightened. "I admit I've—" he placed a hand on Gail's shoulder "—*we've* made mistakes, pretty big ones. I know you worry about us. But we never asked you to do that. Maybe we should've talked to you more."

He sighed. "When your grandfather died fifteen years ago, he left both your dad—" he nodded at Carrie "—and me, money. His will stipulated we had to use the money to buy property. We bought a house here in Gilmartin, which we've rented out since then. That money has been placed into a fund, earmarked for our retirement."

Holy shit. What? Why couldn't he have told her this sooner?

Rheo massaged her temples. "And the money you borrowed from me?"

Ed looked embarrassed. "We knew we couldn't have access to the retirement fund because we'd spend it, so we put it in an inaccessible account. Asking you to help us when we ran short was our only option." He shrugged. "You'll inherit the house one day, so you'll get your money back."

Aaargggghhhhh! So much angst and annoyance could've been avoided if they'd communicated better. "Have you told Paddy this?" she demanded.

Ed snorted. "I tried, but she wasn't prepared to listen. And you know how she sometimes only hears what she wants. I think that happened when I asked her whether she had a will."

"My dad says she likes thinking badly of him and you," Carrie said. She looked at Ed. "Your brother John died while you and Dad lived, and she's never quite forgiven either of you for that."

Was that true? She'd known Paddy preferred John's ambition, but did Paddy feel like *that*? If she did, then maybe Rheo didn't know her grandmother as well as she thought.

"She's goddamn stubborn," Rheo said, shaking her head. "And too set in her ways."

Three sets of eyebrows rose as they all looked at her. Rheo lifted her hands. "What?" she demanded.

"That's the first time we've heard you criticize Paddy," Carrie replied. "Normally, you're her biggest cheerleader."

It was a fair comment, but lately, she'd gained a different perspective on her grandmother. "I love her, but I'm terrified to tell her I screwed up. I shouldn't be this scared of her," Rheo admitted. "If I felt more secure about her love, this wouldn't be as big an issue."

Carrie nodded. "You've always put her on a pedestal, Rheo. You're learning she's a flawed human. We're all flawed, Rhee," Carrie continued. "It makes us what we are and gives us space to change and grow."

Rheo wrinkled her nose. "I don't want another family feud, Carrie."

"And Paddy can start a fight in an empty room," Carrie added. For a full minute, nobody had a reply to her pithy comment.

"Anyway, we were talking about you returning to work, Rheo," Gail said, breaking the silence. "What do you need to return?"

It was nice they were taking an interest. Also a little strange.

"Fletch thinks I need confidence. He thinks that if I succeed at something I hate and suck at, then I can only succeed at something I like and am good at."

"He sounds like a smart guy," Gail commented.

He was.

"So, what do you hate?" Carrie asked. "We could go rock climbing? What about a three-day hike? Kayaking?"

Rheo shuddered. "No, no, and *no*. But Fletch thinks I should enter Gilmartin's Mud Race, the fun one, this weekend," Rheo added, putting as much disdain into her voice as she could manage.

"Oh, you'd hate that!" Carrie cackled.

She would.

"And are you going to do it?" Ed asked.

That would be a hard no.

"I'll do it with you!" Carrie cried, clapping her hands and wiggling her butt in the chair. Nobody should be this excited about doing a mud race. *Ever.* "Would Abi like to do it with us?"

Another hard no.

"I'm not doing it," she told Carrie, but her cousin had the same *I'm not listening to you* expression she remembered from when they were girls.

"You have to live beyond your comfort zone," Carrie insisted.

"Why does going beyond my comfort zone mean me having to get muddy, sweaty, and breathless?"

Carrie rolled her eyes. "Do I really need to explain that to you?"

Because a mud race was everything she hated? And that if she finished the race, if she didn't quit, there would be some measure of pride at knowing she'd completed something she loathed.

"I don't think we've done anything like this together," Carrie said, sounding ridiculously happy. "Oh, this *is* going to be great!"

No, it wasn't, but Rheo couldn't take away her excitement by telling her there was an ice cube's chance in a fucking volcano that she was going to climb over obstacles and run through mud.

Gail started to clear the plates and Carrie stood to help. Carrie's phone buzzed. Rheo looked down and saw Fletch's name light up her screen. So Fletch could text Carrie but not her? *Nice.*

Carrie read the message and looked at Rheo. "They'll be here in a couple of hours," she quietly told Rheo.

"They?"

"Fletch is bringing his friend, his expedition doctor, Seb Michaels, with him," Carrie replied, sounding less than impressed.

God, Fletch texting Carrie instead of her hurt so goddamn much.

"Did he text you?" Carrie asked.

Rheo shook her head.

"I don't know why he's acting like this," Carrie told her, looking genuinely confused. "He's normally so upfront."

Rheo didn't understand either, but she wasn't going to wait around for him. She was going to take a shower, go to bed, and in the morning, she'd deal with Fletch.

She looked at Carrie. "He's got a key. You don't have to wait up for him."

"I know, but I will. Do you want me to pass on a message?" she asked.

Rheo shook her head. By saying nothing, he'd told her a lot.

Thirteen

Rheo heard heavy footsteps in the hallway and recognized them as Fletch's. His bulk filled the doorway to her room. He quietly closed the door, and walked over to the bed, sitting on the strip of mattress next to her. His hand brushed over her hair, and she shivered as his fingers trailed down the bare skin of her arm.

"I'm sorry," he whispered.

Rheo rolled over to face him, and in the semidarkness, saw the deep frown lines between his eyes. He looked tired but smelled great. God, she'd missed him. It was hard to keep her hands off him, so she scooted over to put some space between them. Her plan backfired because he lay down next to her, heat rolling off him. She held herself rigid, resisting the temptation to scoot over to him, to put her bare leg over his, to fling her arm across his T-shirt-covered chest. To kiss her way down his throat, to pull down his boxer shorts and take him in her hand to remind him of what he'd missed.

But she wouldn't. He couldn't ignore her for days and then slip back into her bed and pretend nothing happened.

Fletch rested his forehead against hers, his toothpaste-fresh breath hitting her lips. His stubble was a little longer than usual, and his hair was damp.

"I know I was a jerk, Rhee. We don't even have to make love, I just want to hold you."

Big of him. She bunched her fists. "Did you sleep with anyone else while you were away?" she demanded. She needed to know—she couldn't think until he told her.

Shocked silence hovered between them. "What the *fuck*? No, of course I didn't!"

A little tension dissolved, but she wasn't about to let him off the hook. "It's a fair question, Fletcher."

He raked his hand through his hair, rolled over to face her, and laid a gentle hand on her hip. "Rhee, I was busy doing shit."

"Too busy to send me a message? Just a 'hey' or an 'I'll be back soon'?"

"I'm not used to checking in, Rheo, it's not something I think to do."

Maybe, or he could be bullshitting her big-time. Maybe a little of the first, a lot of the second?

God, she hated feeling confused. Fletch's thumb found a strip of bare skin between the band of her sleeping shorts and her vest, and he painted fire on that square inch of flesh.

She wanted to *punch* him for ghosting her and then crawling back into her bed, his roving hand hinting that he wanted sex. How dare he!

She was about to kick him out when she realized that,
shit, nothing *had* happened between them *but* sex. He'd told
her he wasn't into commitment or settling down, wasn't the
type to fall in love, but here she was, annoyed because she
wanted more and he didn't. That wasn't fair; he didn't owe
her anything.

He'd made her no promises…

And why should she deprive herself of awesome sex? If
that was all she could get from him, she'd take it.

She was desperate to bury her nose in his neck and slide
her leg over him, but because she didn't want to cave so
soon, she told him her parents' van was in his parking space.

"I noticed," he replied, sounding amused. "Carrie said
you had quite a conversation over dinner."

Rheo lifted her shoulder. Moonlight streamed into the
room, but she noticed the concern on his face. "It wasn't
as bad as I expected. I got a few things off my chest. They
did too. They explained I don't need to be as concerned
about them as I've been. It was…" she looked for the word
"…cathartic."

"I'm glad." He shuffled closer, and his bare hand slipped
under the band of her shorts to cup her ass. "You smell so
good," he murmured. "Carrie told me she's going to do the
mud race with you."

Why did everyone assume that her running in the stupid race was a certainty? Yes, she understood why they all
thought she *should* do it, but it didn't mean she was going to.

Rheo snorted. "There's no way Competitive Carrie will

stick at the back of the field to hang with me. I give her a hundred yards before she loses patience."

"You're being kind. I give her fifty," Fletch replied, laying his mouth on her cheekbone. He held it there before speaking again. "I'm proud of you for doing this, Rhee. I know it's not easy for you."

Why was Fletch, and her family, only proud of her when she did the things they liked, activities they approved of? What if she decided, instead of this obstacle race, she wanted to learn calligraphy or how to build a robot? Would they be as proud of her then? Why did their approval come with strings?

She wanted to ask Fletch, but knew it wasn't wise. She could enjoy his body, but she needed to keep her emotional distance. He was her lover, not her soft place to land. His recent actions made that crystal clear.

All she could do was enjoy him and the delicious night. Warm air flowed into her room through the open window, and the gorgeous scent of Fletch's citrus shower gel and Paddy's roses drifted up her nose. Fletch lay next to her, hard and warm and exceptionally masculine. It was a night for lovers, and she was determined to enjoy it.

Rheo lifted her hand, stroking her thumb over his sexy bottom lip. He sighed against her skin, and his eyes fluttered closed.

"I love the way you touch me," Fletch murmured. "If all you did tonight was touch me like that, just on my lip, I'd be happy."

No, he wouldn't. Not really. Neither would she. She wanted more…

Rheo licked her bottom lip. She felt slightly buzzed, and even hotter than she'd been ten seconds before.

"I want to make love to you, Rhee," Fletch told her, the tips of his fingers digging deeper into the skin of her ass. "I want to kiss every inch of you, make you come on my tongue. Then I want to make you come again when I'm buried balls deep inside you."

Lust shot through her like a rocket through space.

Would he always have this power over her, the ability to make her wet and desperate with just a few words? With just a sentence or two, he'd propelled her into the carnal, all her thoughts about her feelings slipping away like the sleeping shorts he pushed down her hips.

Fletch pulled her vest up and over her head, threw it across the room, and Rheo lifted her mouth to find his tongue and slide hers against it. Needing more, her hands streaked over his chest, up and under his T-shirt—it needed to go, immediately—and she slung her thigh over the erection tenting his shorts. So hard, so deliciously hard.

Blood roared through her head as they kissed, desperation too. Rheo pulled her mouth off his, sucked in some air, and dived in for more. Their kiss turned fierce, then ferocious. His hand kneaded her breast, pinched her nipple, and he rolled it between his fingers. His hand dived between her legs, and he parted her folds, seeking her clit. When he hit her most sensitive spot, she lifted her hips off the bed, pushing into him. She knew if he slid even one finger into

her, she would come. She teetered on the edge already and
didn't want to…

Not yet.

Shaking, she pulled his T-shirt up his chest, revealing his
ridged stomach. Fletch used his core muscles to do another
half sit-up, pulling the fabric over his head with a rough
movement. His shorts followed and fell off the side of the bed
to the floor. Rheo knew he could take her, slide into her,
and they'd rock each other to an orgasm—hot, fast, intense.

And that was what she needed. She couldn't handle slow
and sweet tonight. She needed fast, hard, and quick, a physical reminder to mirror their intense, electric, lightning-fast
connection.

Rheo straddled his hips and dragged her wet flesh, aching for him, across his dick until their breaths became moans
and moans morphed into desperation. There was no need to
wait, so Rheo pulled him back with her hand and sank onto
him inch by gorgeous inch. She pushed her aching breasts
into his chest and rested her lips on his.

"I need to come, Fletch, hard and fast," she muttered
against his mouth.

It was such a lie; she needed so much more. She needed
him to love her, to be in her life, to be the missing piece
to complete her puzzle. She *needed* him. In every way that
counted, and a million others she wasn't aware of yet.

But this, having him inside her, rocking his hips, hitting
that spot deep inside that caused her eyes to cross, was all
she had.

She had tonight. She'd take it.

So Rheo clenched her internal muscles, slipped her tongue into his mouth, and took the one thing he could give her.

She took him.

After eating at the Italian place in town, Rheo and Fletch said goodnight to Ed and Gail in the driveway and walked to the back of the house, following Carrie and Seb into the kitchen. Rheo kicked off her wedges, accepted Carrie's quick, unexpected hug, and said goodnight to Seb.

She watched Seb's retreating back and bit down on the inside of her lip. He was a nice guy, and she wondered how Fletch had described their relationship to him. Was she a hookup or a friends-with-benefits deal?

Or was she someone he could come to love?

She was so tired of being an emotional yo-yo—up, down, rolled up, put away. Rinse. Repeat.

Last night she'd tried to treat Fletch as a casual lover, and for about five seconds, it worked. Their first round of sex was fast and furious, and burned the anger and resentment away. But instead of turning over to go to sleep or leaving her bed, he'd—damn him—pulled her onto his lap and cuddled her. His one big hand held her head to his chest, and the other stroked her naked body from shoulder to calf.

They stayed like that—her curled up against his chest, encased within his strength and solidity, his cheek resting on her hair—for ages. But then she felt him stir, and his hand moved to her breast and his thumb drifted over her nipple.

He'd taken forever to love her, to explore every inch of her, to *worship* her. Every touch was deliberate, every kiss infused with intensity. When he brought her—hours, years later—to a soul-shattering climax, she understood, in a primal way, the phrase "to make love."

She fell asleep, wrapped in his arms, a contented smile on her face. Because there was no way a man could spend so much concentrated time loving her, *revering* her, without feeling *something* more.

She didn't care how much more; she'd take it. She'd take anything he could give her.

But when she woke up this morning, he was gone, and he stayed that way.

Fletcher rubbed the back of his neck and Rheo knew he was looking for an excuse to leave the kitchen. He'd been unapproachable all night, so much so that even Gail—Queen of Small Talk—gave up on him.

And how weird was it that he'd met her parents? It was usually such a big step in a relationship. Theoretically, he and her parents had lots in common—traveling, van life, *her*— but him ignoring her put their backs up. As a result, everyone's interactions were stiff and awkward.

What the hell was going on with him?

"I've decided I'm going to talk to Paddy," she told him, pulling two glasses and a bottle of bourbon from the cupboard. She poured a shot into each glass and handed one to Fletch.

C'mon, Fletch, give me something. *A hint of a smile, the tiniest amount of encouragement.*

But his expression didn't change.

"Good idea," he replied.

Really? That was it? "I like Seb," she told him. "He's quiet but witty. What's the beef between him and Carrie?"

"It's their business," Fletch laconically replied, leaning his shoulder into the fridge. Rheo wanted to hit him. But she also wanted to reach into his rib cage, grab his heart, and shake it around, while demanding the return of the funny and warm man she'd shared this house with. This cool, calm, confident stranger was irritating.

"I'm going to my room," Fletch said, looking grim.

His room.

He straightened, and Rheo grabbed his hand. He tried to tug his hand from her grip, but she held on.

"No, we're going to talk," she told him.

He shrugged. "So talk." He glanced at his watch. "But can you make it quick? I have some emails I need to send tonight."

Swear to God, she was going to stab him with a fork. "You're being an asshole, Wright," she snapped. "You've been avoiding me, and we either slug it out here, running the risk of being interrupted, or we take this into the garden."

Fletch looked at her with cool green eyes. "What's there to say?"

Rheo met the challenge in his eyes with a lifted chin. "Here or outside?"

Fletch sighed, and gestured to the kitchen door. Rheo followed him to the now finished gazebo, under which she'd placed a pretty wooden bench. She'd planted clematis in each of the four pots, and in a few summers, the creeper would provide a lovely shaded canopy under which Paddy could sit. But tonight, beyond the wooden beams, icy stars lay on a black velvet sky.

It was a lovely night, one made for romance and hot kisses, for naked bodies and desperate mouths. But since Fletch seemed desperate to avoid talking, all she'd get, if she was lucky, was stilted conversation.

"I'm not going to ask you what I've done wrong, because this is all you," Rheo told him, sitting on the bench and placing her leg over her knee. "*You* left for Portland. I thought everything was fine, and you didn't contact me once. *You* came back from Portland, made love to me, cuddled me, made love to me again, and acted like it was your last night on earth. Then you sneaked out of the room when I was asleep. *You* returned as late as you possibly could today to avoid me. Do you want to tell me why?"

She noticed his hesitation and watched as he tried to formulate a lie she'd believe. "Don't make this situation worse by trying to bullshit me, Wright," she snapped.

He leaned against a wooden pillar, and this time the structure didn't budge. "It was time to put some distance between us," he admitted.

"And you thought ignoring me was a good way to do that?"

"I had things to do in Portland and didn't think I needed to check in with you, to tell you where I was and what I was doing."

Rheo stared at him, not knowing how to respond. He was, after all, speaking the truth. They'd never discussed any sort of commitment.

Something flashed in his eyes, but in the light of the weak half-full moon, she couldn't tell if it was regret or irritation.

"I'm sorry I hurt you by not getting in touch," Fletch said.

He sounded distant and unapproachable, a stranger. Not someone she'd made love to morning and night, and sometimes during the day, for the last six weeks.

Rheo wanted to shout at him, demand he engage, but she couldn't help wondering if she'd just read him catastrophically wrong. Was this on her? Had she projected her feelings onto him last night and this morning and over their whole time together here at the Pink House? He hadn't promised her anything, never hinted at having deeper feelings. She was the one who'd slipped into love…

But she couldn't help feeling that if she dug a little deeper, pushed a little harder, she'd find the man she'd come to love behind this cool stranger. Was she really missing something or was she clutching at straws?

She was tired of his yo-yoing, she *had* to know.

"Talk to me, Fletch," she implored. "Come out from behind that wall and engage with me."

He slid his hands into the pockets of his shorts and lifted one shoulder. "Why? What's the point, Rheo?"

"The point is we are friends, lovers, and now you're behaving like a dick!" She stood in front of him, and placed a hand on his bare, muscled forearm. God, he felt amazing. She wished she didn't love touching him so much.

He looked at his watch again, and Rheo's core temperature rose. Oh, to hell with pussyfooting around, what did she have to lose?

"Over the last few weeks, you've become my friend as well as my lover," Rheo told him. "I've told you things I've never told anyone before. You've become my sounding board and my compass point, someone whose opinion I greatly value."

"That's not my problem—"

She didn't give him a chance to finish his dismissive statement, choosing to thump his arm with her fist. "For one minute, stop being a jerk and talk to me! You've always been so upfront with me. Just be honest, dammit!"

Fletch grabbed her upper arms with his bigger hands, his grip not hard enough to hurt. Hunger and frustration replaced the ice in his moss-green eyes.

"Okay, so what *is* the point, Rheo? What's the point of trying to be friends when all of this—" he lifted one hand to point at the house behind her "—all of what we have *has* to end? I'm trying to put distance between us so we can slide out of each other's lives, but you're determined to fight it."

"I'm trying to understand—"

"Well, do you know what I understand?" he demanded, his voice rough. "We're having a fling, Rheo, it's nothing more than a brief physical connection! I'm sorry you think I'm someone special, but I'm *not*. You're just using that as an excuse to justify our hot meaningless sex."

Oh, hell no, that wasn't fair! The connection they'd made wasn't meaningless. Something existed between them, something he was now trying to deny.

But it glowed. Brightly. And last night she'd felt its light bathing her skin, filling every inch of her.

"C'mon, Fletch."

"I'm being honest, Rheo, isn't that what you wanted?"

Yes, but…

"Even if there was a deeper connection between us, and there's *not*, you're leaving Gilmartin. Soon you'll be at your desk, working ten-hour days. I have to leave too, but I'll be on the opposite side of the country from you, planning my next long-ass expedition, trying to raise sponsorship, training, my entire focus on my work. We'll be six hours and a million light years apart!"

He dropped his hands and linked them behind his head, frustration bubbling over. She'd pulled the cork and his words flowed. "You want a different life than I do, Rheo. We are fundamentally incompatible for anything longer than a fling. We only hooked up because we happened to be in the same place at the same time."

She wanted to protest, but he didn't give her a chance to speak.

"I like everything you don't. Living on the road, seeing what's around the next corner. You need to be in the same place, doing the same job, day in and day out. You need stability, I need freedom. We were always going our separate ways, Rheo. How could you forget?"

She hadn't. Not for one minute. But she imagined they'd keep in touch, that they'd talk and maybe even meet up again.

He caught something on her face, a look in her eyes, and he released a harsh laugh. "And yeah, okay, I admit it, I did ghost you because I felt like we needed to put some distance between us. I came to you last night to apologize, but I can't keep my hands off you." He exhaled sharply. "But, Jesus,

I know it can't work, and I was hoping you'd get there on your own!"

She hadn't considered wedding dresses or a honeymoon in Bali, but she hadn't thought their relationship would end with him treating her like she was an STD he wanted to avoid. And how dare he decide on their future without her input!

"What I know, for sure, Fletcher, is that I am sick of you pulling me closer and pushing me away. One minute you're all about the sex, the next you're acting like you never want to let me go," she told him, just managing to hold on to her dignity. "Opening up one minute, ignoring me the next. And if you thought our situation was becoming too intense, we could've sat down and discussed it. All you needed to do was tell me you felt uncomfortable and that you wanted to slam on the brakes."

Embarrassment skittered across his face, and Rheo knew she'd scored a direct hit. "All I wanted was a little respect, Fletch."

"Rheo… *Fuck*. I just—" Fletch said, running his hands through his hair.

No, he'd said more than enough. She now understood his position. And as he said, it was light-years away from hers.

"Thanks for filling me in on where you stand," she told him, keeping her voice steady.

She turned and walked away, desperate not to cry. When her foot hit the first of the steps leading to the kitchen door, he called her name in a hoarse voice. She slowly turned and lifted her hands in a *What now?* gesture.

He waved to the bench. "Just come back and let's talk, okay?"

Rheo's eyebrows rose. "Now you want to talk?" She shook her head in disbelief. "Yeah, I think you've said everything you need to, Wright. Save your breath."

Rheo, her heart cracking, climbed the steps to the kitchen and slipped inside the house. They said you should never ask a question unless you absolutely wanted to hear the truth, and she'd relearned that lesson tonight.

Fletch didn't love her. Couldn't. And he never would.

She hated this.

No, she *fucking* hated this.

Rheo gripped the slippery net and tried to haul her body up it. Her muscles screamed. She glared at the brown legs of a ten-year-old flying past her and couldn't work out why she'd said yes to competing in this stupid race. She was covered in mud—there was mud in her teeth for God's sake! Every muscle in her body begged her to stop and she knew her slow pace was irritating Carrie. Carrie wanted to fly but felt honorbound to stay with Rheo. If she could raise the energy, she still wouldn't care.

She was only twenty minutes into the race, and she was over it. This was *so* not her thing.

Rheo rolled over the top of the net and dropped into the ankle-deep mud. Another wave of sludge invaded her sneakers, and she closed her eyes. How much longer? And could she just die here?

Carrie grabbed her hand and pulled her along the slushy

track, forcing Rheo into a half run. Carrie, unlike her, looked reasonably clean. Her legs were a bit muddy, but from her navel up she looked shower-fresh. In fact, everyone but Rheo looked reasonably clean.

She looked like a swamp witch.

Rheo told Carrie to go on ahead—she was dying to, and off she trotted, a perfect little pony. Rheo's mood was as foul as this mud; she was far out of her comfort zone, dirty, sweaty, and tired. And furious with Fletch.

Soul deep, catastrophically angry. Because, by shutting her out of his life, he'd made her feel ten years old again, trying to fit into her parents' lives.

Rheo pushed her hand into her side, trying to massage away a stitch. In the distance, Carrie exchanged a quip with an older man and their laughter drifted back to her. Ed and Gail, standing on the sidelines, shouted something at Carrie, who dropped into a quick curtsy. Emotions from her childhood welled up. It was always them and her—she was little Rheo again, her nose pressed against the window, looking in.

Last night, with Fletch, she'd felt out of the loop yet again, on the outside of his life asking to be let in. She'd become an unwanted presence for him, a complication, a *What the fuck do I do with her now?* problem.

Rheo looked at the tunnel she needed to crawl through and shook her head. What else would she have to do before she could shower? At the end of her rope, physically and mentally, she fought the urge to walk away.

She desperately wanted to.

She *could*. No one held a gun to her head, it wasn't a case of life or death, and judging by the concerned looks her family kept sending her, they were surprised she'd lasted this long. They were watching her, trying not to be obvious about it, wondering whether this was the point when she threw in the towel.

They expected her to, she could see it on their faces.

What if she did? Why did she have to run a stupid race to prove she was brave and confident and in control?

She'd come a long way over the past six weeks, admittedly with Fletch's guidance. She wasn't so panic-stricken and could look at the future with a measure of calm. She'd gained a measure of confidence from knowing such a masculine, rugged man wanted her, and that confidence seeped into the rest of her life. Through talking to Fletch, she'd come to face her demons and found ways to dodge them.

She'd come a long way and she'd grown up. A little.

She liked herself more than she did seven weeks ago, the biggest revelation of all.

"C'mon, Rheo!" her dad shouted, his hands around his mouth.

Rheo dropped to her knees, released a series of f-bombs, and crawled through the mud-filled tunnel. It smelled like dirt and stanky water and sweat. She emerged and she pulled in a couple of deep breaths of fresh air.

This wasn't fun and she didn't want to do it anymore. Rheo lifted her T-shirt and wiped the sweat off her forehead before realizing she'd substituted sweat for mud.

Yuck.

She was done. She didn't need to prove anything…not to them. They should love her no matter what, no matter how she approached life and its challenges. She could complete this race, she knew she could. She could stomp through more mud and cross another ditch. She might have to ask for a heart transplant at the end of it, but she would finish.

But why should she have to do this categorically stupid race to prove she was confident and in control? She was making a point to *them*, not herself. She already had faith in what she could do.

And because she did, she would go back to the UN and she would *do* her job to the best of her ability. If she hit the UN's high standard, excellent. If she didn't, she would make another plan and find something else to do. She was smart and she was strong and she didn't need Fletch, Paddy, or her parents' approval.

Rheo slapped her hands on her thighs and looked over to where the onlookers stood, her eyes drawn to two tall men. Sunlight bounced off Fletch's hair, more gold than blond in the sunlight. Neither he nor Seb, who'd joined his team at the last minute, looked like they'd completed a twelve-mile obstacle course.

The bastards.

Her eyes connected with Fletch's, and they stared at each other. Across the mud and grass, blue slammed into green, and the shouts of the onlookers and the music from huge speakers faded away. Fletch lifted one eyebrow. He knew she was about to walk away, that she was done. Disappointment and irritation flickered over his face.

He'd expected her to quit. Wasn't surprised. And at that moment, one of the few times in her life, Rheo hated her predictability.

No, damn him. She categorically refused to give him the satisfaction of being right.

She wasn't done, not quite yet.

Lifting her head, she scowled at him before turning back to the track. There weren't many obstacles left, one of which was a rope climb, up and over an inclined wooden wall. She would get over that fucking wall if it killed her.

The resolution to finish the damn course now had nothing to do with her needing confidence or being out of her comfort zone; she simply needed to show Fletch he was wrong. She had grit. She didn't fold. She was mentally tough and stronger than he believed her to be.

Pissy? Absolutely. Prissy? Not so much.

Fletch might be a big-time explorer who'd crossed jungles and glaciers. Carrie might be an adventurous wild girl, and Rheo's parents might be wanderers. But Rheo possessed determination in spades. She'd studied her ass off to get her master's in romance languages, and she'd worked damn hard to build a reputation for consistency and accuracy in the UN Interpretation Service. She'd made a home and created the life she needed, a life that made her feel secure and stable.

Sure, it wasn't *their* life, but it took hard work and persistence. If completing a stupid obstacle course covered in mud showed them—not herself, *them*—that she could do anything she put her mind to, then she'd do it.

She'd do it even if it killed her. And it very well might.

Rheo finished second to last in the fun race that afternoon, but Fletch thought it was a miracle she'd finished at all. As he'd watched her white-knuckle her way through the race, he'd been convinced, a few times, she'd throw in the towel.

But Rheo surprised him by carrying on. Though, God, he couldn't believe anyone could take so long to climb that rope wall. Rheo's arms looked lovely, but she had the upper body strength of a noodle.

He'd needed to catch up on work, so after watching Rheo stumble over the finish line, he'd returned to the Pink House and spent the next four hours on his laptop, answering emails and catching up with his production company CEO. He was tired. And hungry. Walking down the stairs of the Pink House, he frowned at the lack of noise. He'd expected Rheo's parents and Carrie to be in the kitchen or the sitting room, catching up over a bottle of wine, but when he stuck his head into the living room, library, and study, they were all empty. In the kitchen, he noticed a note propped against an open wine bottle.

Ed, Gail, Seb, and I have gone out for a drink at Diego's. Meet us there!

C, xoxo

The last place he wanted to be was in a noisy bar, especially since he knew it was karaoke night. Carrie loved karaoke and would be there until the bar closed, and so, he imagined, would Ed and Gail. Seb, a lot more reserved, would sit in the corner and make jibes at Carrie for being an attention seeker. He didn't want to be with them. He wanted to be with Rheo.

After pouring a glass of wine, Fletch walked out the back door to the gazebo, thinking of his and Rheo's uncomfortable conversation the night before. He'd spoken the truth—they were too different and couldn't have a relationship going forward. Flying in to see each other, taking a weekend here, a week there? No, it was impossible, and because he'd always want more, he'd be constantly frustrated and miserable. It was far better to end it now, before they managed to hurt each other more.

But he wasn't proud of how he'd laid it on the line. He wasn't used to heart-to-heart discussions or having his feet held to a conversational fire, and he'd floundered. But he should have had a fucking conversation with her, and discussed his doubts.

And ghosting her had been a dick move.

Rheo sat on the bench, her bare feet on the seat, her arms around her knees. Of course, she was here. He'd subconsciously expected her to be. She looked pale and shattered, and he suspected every muscle in her body was on fire. He wished he could massage her from tip to toe before making slow and tender love to her.

But he knew that after everything they'd said to each other

yesterday—and him burning all their bridges by being an asshole—there was no going back.

Yet he couldn't stay away.

He leaned against the same pole as he had last night. "How are you feeling, Rhee?" he asked.

She scowled. "Like I ran five miles without training. I think I've pulled every muscle in my body."

He winced. "Well done for finishing."

When her eyes connected with his, he clocked the heat in hers. He was in the path of an incoming missile and there was nowhere to run.

"Don't patronize me, Fletch."

What? Where did that come from? He was genuinely proud of her for finishing, as he told her.

She shook her head, disbelieving. He had never seen her look so remote. They needed to cross their t's and dot their i's, but he didn't know where to start, or even how to start.

Rheo dropped her legs and looked up at him, her expression hard. "So, is this where you tell me that I did great, that I can walk back into my job feeling massively more confident because I finished that stupid race? Screw you, Fletch, I didn't need a race to feel like that."

Huh? "You finished the race. Surely you feel some sense of achievement?"

"I didn't *need* to finish the race, I was good with quitting and happy with my decision. Then you looked at me, and I wanted to show you, only you, that you were wrong about me. I have grit and determination—lots of it—for what I want to do. All I needed was for you, and them, my parents and Carrie, to hold my hand and tell me that I'd be fine, that I would figure it out, that I had this."

He felt lost. "I thought you were amazing out there. I am so incredibly proud of you."

She sent him a thin smile. "But it would've meant more if you'd been proud of me whatever way the chips fell. If you'd supported me when I told you, and everyone, that I didn't want to do that stupid fucking race, *that* would've been brilliant. But, no, you couldn't do that. You, like everyone else in my family, only respect grit and determination and self-respect when you can relate to it.

"Tell me, Fletcher, how would you feel if I demanded you do a speech in French to bigwigs of a production company, right now, when you've never spoken the language before?" she asked.

Shit. *Shit.*

Her words were a spear through his heart. She was right, dammit. Not only had he botched up the end to their relationship, he'd pushed her into his world, confident in his belief that he knew what she needed. He *was* a patronizing prick.

"I'm so sorry, Rhee. I'm sorry I made you feel less than, like my approval was contingent on your completing that race. I never doubted your determination, Rhee. It's one of the many things I lo— like about you."

She narrowed her eyes, unimpressed by his statement. Admittedly, maybe it was too little too late. "You sure don't act like you lo—" Rheo deliberately cut the word off, too sharp to have missed his earlier slip of the tongue "—*like* me."

He looked her in the eye and didn't pull away. He owed her that.

"So, are you finally admitting there are some feelings between us?"

"Yes."

He couldn't tell her he was fathoms deep in love with her, that he wanted to stay but couldn't.

"Feelings that are deeper than they should be," he quietly admitted. "Feelings I should have talked to you about, instead of ghosting you."

What else could he say? It was the truth.

But their feelings—love, like, lust, need, want—didn't change a damn thing. Nothing would keep them together when they would be, geographically, miles apart. Continents apart. Across the world apart.

Knowing what he wanted, what he couldn't have, sent anger streaking through his soul. "How does any of this help when we can't be with each other? How does it solve the fact that we are diametrically opposite people who love different things?"

She shrugged.

"What's the fucking point of feeling like this when nothing can come of it, Rheo?" he shouted. He hauled in a deep breath and lowered his voice. "How the hell do you think we could make a relationship work? You're not naive, Rheo. You can't wave a magic wand and make it all work out."

"I—"

No, he couldn't do this. She needed to understand it wasn't possible. "I will *not* give up my work for you, Rheo.

I wouldn't do that for anyone. And if I won't do that for you, I sure as hell can't expect you to do it for me! My expeditions run for nine months a year. You'd be on your own."

Rheo's eyebrows rose and she started to speak, but Fletch refused her the chance. They were an iceberg hitting a canoe. A typhoon hitting a wooden fishing hut. They'd end up hating each other, and he wouldn't do that to them…he couldn't. He'd tried to minimize how he felt about her, and pushed his feelings away. Tried ghosting her. Nothing worked. But he was dman certain that she'd come to loathe him if he loved her, but kept leaving her.

He couldn't live in the world knowing Rheo hated him.

"I will never be a nine-to-five husband. You need one of those. You need someone who wants a stable life, who is predictable. Someone who will be there every night, over weekends and holidays. I'm not that man."

Rheo wasn't crying. Thank God—her tears would drop him to his knees. All she did was watch and wait. And after a few moments, she spoke again. "Are you done?"

He nodded and rubbed his hands over his face. He couldn't tell her how much he wanted her to be there when he returned from an expedition, to sink into her world of comfort and stability for a few weeks or months. Rheo welcoming him home was the ultimate prize, but he couldn't ask her to hang around *waiting* for him, her life on hold…

God, it hurt.

"There you go again, telling me what I need and want," she stated, her voice cool. "For someone who's conquered mountains and jungles, lived through blizzards, and pushed himself to his physical limits, you're quite the coward, aren't you?"

Her words punched him in the chest, knocking the wind out of him. He couldn't answer. He could only stare at her, his mouth open in shock.

"You can do, have done, all these amazing things, but you are useless at being emotionally brave. I'm much better at that than you."

How so? he wanted to ask, but his words were burrs in his throat.

"I've pulled myself out of...well, not a black spot, but out of a deep rut. You coming into my life helped, but I've made a lot of progress on my own. I've reconnected with my family—they still drive me nuts, but I'm learning to live with them—and I hope I won't be as judgmental of them going forward. I'm going to return to my job, because I love it, hoping I can do it to the standard they require. If I can't, I will find something else," she told him.

How could she sound so calm when he had a million fire ants crawling under his skin?

"I never asked you to give up exploring for me, Fletch. It's not something I'd ever expect you to do. Loving you— and yes, I'm going there!—means accepting exploration is a huge part of you, accepting I'd only have minimal time with you." She shrugged and sent him a sad smile. "The thing is, I'd rather have minimal time with you than no time at all. I might not be able to scale mountains, cross raging rivers, or even complete a stupid-ass race without doing myself a permanent injury, but I'm brave enough to be honest, and courageous enough to recognize love when it drops into my life."

Fletch's world now rested on shifting ground. He wanted to apologize and explore this new world she'd introduced him to, but another part of him, the biggest part, was terrified of taking her hand. Terrified of taking the first step into a new landscape. A life, emotionally connected but physically apart.

Because he was petrified, at the end of his emotional rope, and unable to deal with any of this, he uttered words he knew would stop her in her tracks.

"You're not that brave, Rheo! Jesus, do you really think you are?" he asked, hating himself for lashing out, but unable to stop. "You can't even call your grandmother and tell her you're living in her house and that you've been out of work for nearly six months. You say you are being honest, but you're not. Do you *honestly* think you'd be happy with me dropping in and out of your life? You'd resent me. What if we had kids? You'd hate me because I wasn't doing my share. Try being truly honest, Rheo."

She stood up and wrapped her arms around her torso, her hot blue eyes slicing through him. "I'm not an idiot, nor am I blinded by love. I would go into a relationship with you with my eyes wide-open. But you don't love me enough, or at all, and you're not prepared to find a way to make it work. And that's okay, Fletch. There's no rule stating you have to jump in."

Rheo pushed her hair off her face, and he could see she was holding back tears. She forced her mouth into a smile.

"My parents are leaving tomorrow, and I'm catching a ride to the airport with them. I'll be in New York by tomorrow morning."

Wait, hold on! "You can't just dump this on me and walk away, Rheo!"

"Actually, I can, Fletch. All you've said, over and over, is that we won't work," Rheo told him, her expression and voice dignified. "I'm not going to beg you to love me, plead with you to find space for me in your life. I did that with my parents, and I deserve better."

Rheo placed her hand on his arm and stood on her tiptoes to kiss the side of his mouth. When she dropped back to her feet, she squeezed his arm. "Have a good life, Fletch. And, for God's sake, be careful. I couldn't bear it if anything happened to you."

Rheo hauled in a deep breath, turned, and walked away.

And Fletch watched his heart leave with her.

Fourteen

On Rheo's second day back at work, her third Fletch-free day, Nicole assigned her a simultaneous translation for a Spanish delegation taking part in a preliminary discussion on worldwide fishing rights and quotas.

It was, she knew, her boss's way of tossing her into the deep end.

Taking a seat in her booth, Rheo adjusted her microphone and wondered why she wasn't feeling nervous. It could be because, compared to feeling broken-hearted and emotionally shattered, she had no bandwidth left to feel nervous about translating. She missed Fletch with every part of her, from the tips of her toes to the ends of her hair.

Having no memories of being with him in the city, she'd believed she wouldn't miss him as much here, but it didn't make any difference at all. She missed their connection, their conversations—both silly and serious. She longed to hear his voice, be warmed by his laugh. Yes, she missed the sex, but she missed him more.

She missed her friend, her lover, the flip side of her coin.

Rheo looked at her watch, saw she still had five minutes before the meeting started, and put her head in her hands. She wasn't even worried about talking to Paddy anymore; she'd messed up, and Paddy either accepted her explanation or she didn't. Rheo wasn't going to put a knot in her stomach anticipating her grandmother's reaction. She loved Paddy, but she wasn't going to live her life anxious for her grandmother's approval.

Compared to missing Fletch, nothing else affected her emotional landscape. She missed everything about him...

Sure, having a relationship with him would have been difficult. Yes, they wouldn't see each other for months at a time, but what was the alternative? Not seeing each other at all? That was unacceptable to her... But he was terrified of the love she'd offered him.

This was the reality of her life. And it sucked dragon balls.

Rheo checked her watch and looked over the meeting room, wondering why so few people were seated at the desks. The meeting was supposed to start in a few minutes. Pushing back her chair, she popped her head out of the booth and caught the eye of a fellow translator standing in the hallway next to the entrance to his booth, scrolling through his phone.

"Hi, Yusaf." She gestured to her booth. "What's going on? What's the delay?"

He looked up and smiled. "Yeah, one of the members

collapsed and they called an ambulance. Security pushed the meeting back an hour. I'm going to grab a cup of coffee. Would you like to join me?"

His offer surprised her. Before she left, her colleagues avoided her, possibly because they thought her meltdown was contagious. Yusaf's offer meant they'd put her mistakes behind them and moved on. She should too. If she was going to do this job, then she had to *do* her job and stop looking for pitfalls and problems. She had to be all in.

But before she could move forward, there was something she had to do. When it was over, she could start fresh in every way.

She sent Yusaf a smile. "Can I take a rain check?"

She caught the disappointment in his eyes, and a little flash of contempt. He thought she was the Rheo from before. The one who kept herself apart, who didn't bother to engage.

"Yeah, sure," he said in a flat voice. Rheo suspected he wouldn't make the offer again.

As he started to walk away, she grabbed his arm. When their eyes met, she managed a tentative smile. "Please ask me again—I promise to say yes next time. I just need to phone my grandmother. It's something I've been putting off because we're about to have our first argument in…well, the first one ever. I've always looked up to her, and I'm about to disappoint her. She's not going to be pleased."

Yusaf looked surprised, then gratified, to hear her explanation. "The weight of family expectations, huh?"

She nodded, grimacing. "But I'm trying to live my code of what's right and wrong, and not theirs."

"Good luck," he said, smiling. "And we expect to see you at our next poker night, Whitlock."

Damn. "I don't play poker, but I'm willing to learn," she told him.

Yusaf grinned. "Neither do we, to be honest. Mostly we look at cards, throw chips into a pile, and insult each other in ten different languages."

Poker sounded like fun. She needed friends, not only to fill her time but to create a richer, fuller life. Connecting with her coworkers would be a good place to start.

Turning back into her booth, she sat, picked up her cell from her desk, and hit the green button to FaceTime Paddy. Her grandmother answered almost immediately, holding a tumbler in her hand.

Paddy, her white hair immaculately coiffured, and wearing a white open-neck shirt and heavy silver necklace, lifted her drink in greeting. "Darling girl, it's good to see you."

She looked happy and hearty, full of the joy of life, but Rheo was about to ruin her afternoon. Oh, well…

"Why are you looking, as my Texan grandfather used to say, like you hanged the wrong horse thief?"

Courage, Whitlock. Find it and speak.

"I screwed up at work, I had to take a leave of absence, I went to Gilmartin, and lived in the Pink House without your permission for six months." Rheo machine-gunned her words, thinking they'd sound better if she said them fast.

Paddy's expression hardened, and her blue eyes turned frosty. "I saw the viral video, I know you've been away from work, and I sure as hell knew you were living in the Pink

House. I've been many things in my life, my girl, but I am not stupid."

Rheo stared at the screen, trying to take everything in. She understood the individual words, but they didn't make sense. Paddy knew? Everything? Already?

Her grandmother drained her drink and looked around for a waiter. Rheo's eyes widened when she saw a Chris Hemsworth doppelganger, wearing only a pair of swim trunks. Tanned skin and impressive shoulders and biceps. Paddy asked him for another gin and tonic and turned the screen so Rheo could admire his washboard stomach.

"Meet my granddaughter, Harry," Paddy said. "Rheo, this is Harry."

Harry tipped the phone so Rheo wasn't looking at his crotch and grinned, flashing perfectly white, straight teeth. "G'day, Rheo. Your grandmother's told me a lot about you."

Rheo waved at Harry, said hello, and when Paddy turned the camera back onto her lined face, Rheo frowned at her. "Who is Harry and why is he fetching you drinks at what looks like a seaside villa?"

Paddy raised an imperious eyebrow. "Harry is my new friend Stuart's grandson. He's been working on yachts in the Mediterranean. A nice boy," she explained.

Who was Stuart? She'd never heard Paddy mention him before. And today she didn't care. She had bigger things to think about right now. Like…why wasn't Paddy having a shit fit? Paddy wasn't reacting as Rheo expected, and she didn't know how to feel about that.

"What do you mean, you knew about the viral video,

me losing my job, and my six months living in your house, Paddy?" she demanded, noticing staff members were filtering into the meeting room.

"I have alerts on my phone to tell me whenever anything happens at the UN, like a terrorist attack or a bomb threat," Paddy explained. Rheo worked in one of the most secure buildings in the world, but Paddy was worried something would happen to her. "I got numerous alerts about the video and was curious to see what all the fuss was about. I recognized your voice instantly."

Was there anyone who didn't know she was the translator on the viral video? Maybe some horse trader in Mongolia?

Paddy sipped from her glass, and despite her relaxed stance, Rheo knew she was borderline pissed. Paddy didn't like being left out of the loop.

"I made a mistake," Rheo hurriedly explained. "People do make mistakes, Grandmother."

"You don't, Rheo!"

Rheo sucked in a harsh breath. "That's not fair, Paddy. You're putting a hell of a lot of pressure on me. You always have." Rheo pushed her finger and thumb into her eye sockets.

Was she being fair? Probably not. She'd *chosen* to be like Paddy. "I'm allowed to fail, Paddy!"

Paddy drained her G-and-T and slammed the glass on the side table next to her lounger. She released a loud sigh. "Of course you are. Failure is a part of life."

Wait! What? "That isn't something you've told me before."

"Maybe I'm upset because I'm used to you doing everything perfectly. And because I like knowing I don't have to worry about you. I never had to sort you out or run to your rescue. Nobody in this family realizes how much thinking and worrying I do on their behalf."

Paddy was being more dramatic than usual. But since she wasn't yelling or screaming, Rheo would take the win. It was also a good time to go on the offensive.

"While we're talking about sorting things out, you need to resolve the situation between you and my dad," she told Paddy.

Paddy sighed, and she dropped her gaze. Was she embarrassed? Rheo didn't know—she'd never seen Paddy blush before.

"For a few months after our argument, I was convinced he'd been disrespectful by speaking to me about my will. I was furious when he wouldn't apologize. Ed never takes responsibility for his actions, never admits he's wrong."

"He learned that from you," Rheo cheekily stated. She'd never spoken to Paddy like this, frankly and openly. She finally felt like an adult. Sort of.

Paddy picked up her empty glass and rested it against her cheek. For the first time, she looked old and a little frail. "I was sick when your father phoned me. I had the flu and I wasn't myself. Between the meds I was taking, the lack of sleep from coughing, and my high temperatures, I got our conversation wrong."

Wow. "Why didn't you tell him that?"

"I've called myself an idiot, and I know I'm too proud," Paddy reluctantly admitted. "I couldn't find a way to say sorry."

"You pick up the phone, admit you got it wrong, and say

sorry," Rheo told her, not bothering to hide her frustration. Because there had been so much hurt, too much arrogance, and too little understanding—*and no communication!*—her voice rose. "This isn't rocket science, Paddy!"

Then she recalled where she was. She checked that the door was closed and her microphone was switched off. See? She could learn from her mistakes. "You admit what you've done and ask for forgiveness."

"And is that so easy to do, Rheo? Obviously not, because it's taken you six months to tell me you've been living rent-free in the Pink House."

Her words were an excellent counterargument. Rheo didn't have a leg to stand on, so she told Paddy she'd pay her whatever rent she thought was fair. It would bite into her savings, but it was the right thing to do. She was an adult, and she paid her way.

Paddy waved her words away. "Pride is a hell of a thing, my dear, and it always, *always* comes before a fall. You failed and so did I," Paddy quietly stated. "We learn from it and go on. I could make you pay rent for living in my house without my permission—"

"How did you find out, by the way?" Rheo interrupted her.

"Darling, I ruled the town for years," Paddy responded with her confident drawl. "Nobody sneezes without me knowing about it. I received emails and text messages ten minutes after you arrived."

Right. She should've known she wouldn't get away with it, even if the town *had* changed.

"I thought about confronting you, but after getting it

wrong with your father, I didn't want to be estranged from another, and my most beloved, family member. I kept hoping you'd tell me yourself."

Rheo closed her eyes, her anger fading away. "I felt like such a failure, not sure what I was going to do, or even if I'd be able to return to work. I was a leaf caught in a tornado."

Paddy's self-deprecating smile was full of wisdom. "Maybe the lesson we both have to learn is that we are allowed to get things wrong and that failure is a part of life and a way for us to grow."

For all Rheo's life, Paddy had been so confident. She'd never once seen her second-guess herself. This was another version of her grandmother, and Rheo quite liked her.

"Stuart, the wise old man that he is, says we don't grow from success."

Rheo still didn't know who Stuart was, where Paddy had met him, and what role he was playing in her life, and she burned with curiosity. Lover? Friend? Tour guide?

But before she could ask, Paddy spoke again. "You made some mistakes, but it sounds like you've managed to come out the other side without my help and without me telling you what to do. I'm glad, Rheo, because it's important for you to trust yourself and trust your judgment. I think you've relied too heavily on mine up to now."

She had. And Rheo understood Paddy's subtext: her grandmother was an old lady, and she wasn't going to be around forever. It was time for Rheo to grow up and stand on her own two feet. She could do that. While she might still be a little wobbly, at least she was upright.

Forza e coraggio che la vita è un passaggio. She needed strength and courage, because life was a passage she had to navigate.

"You're stubborn and intolerant and demanding," Rheo gently told her.

"I can be. So can you."

It was a fair comment, so Rheo nodded. "Please talk to my dad and apologize, Paddy."

"I will."

Paddy never went back on her word, and a hundred tons lifted off Rheo's shoulders.

"I've fallen in love, Paddy," Rheo told her, thinking she'd tell Paddy everything. Then, after months of distance, they'd both be on the same page. "He's not into my life, I'm not into his, but I'm into him in the biggest way imaginable."

"You're in love with the young man who rented my house? Carrie's friend?"

"His name is Fletcher. He's the last person in the world I should have fallen in love with. He's an adventurer, an explorer, someone who can't sit still or stay in the same place."

Paddy wrinkled her nose. "Darling… I wish I could tell you everything will be all right, but I can't. Sometimes loving someone isn't enough. Sometimes love doesn't work out, and more often than not, there are no happy endings, because life isn't a fairy tale. I think being able to love, being able to connect, and being able to walk away when things are impossible is what's important. That's love, that's truth and that's strength."

It might be, but it still hurt, like a million mini meteor strikes. She kept having to pick up her pieces and glue them into place again. Rinse, repeat. Rheo glanced at her watch and eyed the attendees gathered below. She was out of time.

"I have to get back to work, Paddy."

"You said you were worried about doing your job. Can you do it?"

"Of course I can do my job, Paddy," she replied.

And, at that moment, she sensed the truth in her soul. Here, behind this desk and microphone, was where she belonged. She believed in herself, and her abilities, and her opinion was the only one that mattered.

Rheo pointed a finger at Paddy. "Call my dad."

Paddy pulled a face. "I will invite them to visit me when I return to the States."

No, that wasn't good enough. "You will call him, preferably via video, and you will apologize. I will stay on your case until you do."

Paddy cocked her head to the side. "I see the tables have turned."

They hadn't flipped entirely, neither of them believed that. She'd always love and respect Paddy, and her grandmother would always be protective of her.

Sin che si vive, s'impara sempre. They lived. They learned.

And today they'd met as adults and signed an unspoken agreement to be accountable. Not only to each other, but also to themselves.

Could anything be more worthwhile?

Hanging off the rock face in the Red River Gorge, Fletch attached his carabiner into a hook in the rock face. He briefly looked down and shrugged. He was only a hundred feet up, on a climb called Bedtime for Bonzo. He wasn't fazed. This was a training climb, a way to get him fit for longer, higher, and more extreme peaks. His team was easing him in...

Yet, despite being barely off the ground, he couldn't get enough oxygen into his lungs. The last time he had felt this way was when he was climbing Everest. Comparing this climb to Everest was like putting a bicycle against a Bugatti Veyron.

Why did he feel short of air? Was he getting sick? Was there something wrong with his circulation? Was he sliding back into CFS? Fletch leaned back in his harness and bumped the ball of his hand against his temple. He was fine, just not as fit as he usually was, out of condition.

Pull your head out of your ass and concentrate, Wright.

Fletch pushed his fingers into a crack, looked for a foothold, and didn't find one. He scanned the rock, noticed a ledge, and thought that if he could lunge for it, he could scrabble a few yards up the rock face. As he reached for the ledge, an image of Rheo's bemused face flashed behind his eyes, and he heard her asking him why the hell he was doing this.

He didn't put enough energy behind his effort and missed the ledge, his fingertips scraping along a sharp ridge. He fell fast, waited for the rope to bite, and cursed when his shoulder plowed into the hard rock. He jerked his head back just in time to avoid it bouncing off the rock too.

Shit! Fuck! That hurt. He panted softly, adrenaline and pain coursing through him.

His radio squawked. "You okay, Fletch?"

Pulling out his radio from the pouch behind his ass, he

assured Jason, his belayer and rope master, he was fine. Actually, his shoulder hurt like a bitch, but there was nothing he could do about it right now.

"That was an easy lunge," Jason told him, sounding puzzled. "You should be able to do it in your sleep. What's wrong with you?"

So much, Fletch silently told him.

"I need to take a break," he curtly told Jason. "Give me ten."

Fletch placed his radio back into its pouch, placed his feet against the rock and sat in the harness. He looked at his bleeding fingertips and wiped them on his climbing pants. He tipped his head back and watched the clouds float across the Kentucky sky. He'd just come off a two-month break and should be energized and pumped. His enthusiasm levels should be at an all-time high. But instead of feeling excited, all he felt was flat and hollow, emotionally washed out.

Climbing, exploring, and being outside were what he most enjoyed, what he wanted to do, and where he wanted to be. But it didn't mean as much as it did before he met Rheo. God, he missed her. He missed talking to her, hearing her laugh, his skin buzzing with their sizzling chemistry. Sure, he missed the sex, but he missed the person he was when he was with her. Calm, settled, loved.

She loved him, he didn't doubt it. And he loved her in ways he'd never loved anyone before.

It had taken weeks for him to accept that the strange emotions coursing through his system meant he was in love. He hadn't thought he'd ever experience it. Then he felt pissed he'd fallen in love with a woman who couldn't and wouldn't share this life that was as necessary to him as breathing.

But *was* it? He wasn't having any fun on this trip. Would he feel the same way when he started his next expedition? What was the point of putting them through all the many hardships, pushing themselves and their equipment, if he wasn't excited to be there? If he didn't get the rush of adrenaline, that hit of satisfaction?

Without Rheo in his life, it meant less than it had before. And that made no sense at all.

But she did understand him, and understood exploring was the biggest part of him. She never asked him to give it up; she just asked to love him while he did it. Fletch rested his forehead against the sun-warmed rock and looked through the gap between his knees to the ground below. Nothing made sense anymore, and being alone wasn't what he wanted to be.

He wanted Rheo in his life.

He needed to start his day hearing her voice, even if she was half asleep and it took her a while to wake up. He wanted to end his day telling her about the hawk that buzzed him, that the sky reminded him of her blue eyes. He wanted to hear how her day went, how she was doing at work, whether she'd met anyone important, translated anything interesting.

He hadn't given them a chance, and neither did he give any thought to how they *could* work.

He was an explorer, someone who always found a way through, someone who always had a plan. And a backup plan. And a backup plan for his backup plan.

But with Rheo, he'd just looked at the map and decided

he couldn't succeed, that she was a land that would forever remain unexplored. The lack of action wasn't like him—he didn't give up without trying. He had acted out of character because, while he wasn't scared of getting dinged and dented by Mother Nature, he was protective of his heart.

He was outwardly brave but not, as Rheo informed him, courageous enough to risk being vulnerable.

He'd somehow, without meaning to, found everything he wanted in a woman in one small town in Washington. Whether he was with her or not, whether they talked or not, Rheo held his heart in her hands, and he was at her mercy.

He suddenly knew he wouldn't get back to himself, to enjoy what he did and the life he'd chosen, until he took a chance. Until he figured out a way to make them work.

He might fail—some expeditions did—but he had to try.

He wasn't a goddamn quitter.

"Ready to go, Fletch?" Jason asked, his voice muffled.

Fletch looked down and saw Jason standing on the valley floor below him. He squinted. Despite the distance between them, Jason's worry shimmered off him.

Fletch slashed at his neck and reached behind him to pull out his radio. "I'm calling it, Jase. I'm done."

"Did you hurt yourself?" Jason asked, anxious.

Yes, but not in the way Jason meant. He'd also hurt Rheo, and it would take a long time for him to forgive himself for doing it. If ever. Nobody was allowed to hurt her, including him.

"My head isn't in the right place, so I don't think I should be trying to scale one of the hardest rock faces in the area. I'm putting myself in danger."

Jason didn't reply, but eventually, his radio crackled again. "Fair enough."

He told Fletch to prepare to rappel, and Jason radioed the team who waited at another point in the valley, asking Seb to check Fletch's shoulder. He understood Jason's worry—he never bailed on a challenge. He pushed the envelope and was the person who wanted to go faster, higher, do more, and take bigger risks. His team kept his feet on the ground, not the other way around.

Things were changing.

He was changing.

Even so, he had to consider whether he'd ruined his chances with Rheo by handing her a lot of crap and taking out his fear on her by not treating her well. She would be within her rights to tell him to find Fuck Mountain, climb it, and throw himself off when he reached the summit. As he well knew, choices had consequences, and his decision to run instead of planting his feet and sticking around, might come back to annihilate him.

What would he do then?

One step at a time, Wright. Read the map, plan your route. Take it from there.

When Rheo left Gilmartin for Brooklyn she understood, and accepted, that she would have to make modifications to her very stable, very predictable life. It was safe having a well-oiled life, but it was also damn boring. And keeping busy was one way to get out of her head and stop her thoughts about Fletch—was he okay? Where was he? Had he found another woman to sleep with?

She video-called Abi every day, and she'd joined her colleagues' poker night and enjoyed an evening filled with laughter and losing pretend money. She'd played exceptionally badly and drank too much wine. Because she was a horrendous cook, she'd signed up for cooking classes. And a night class to learn Mandarin was an option. She needed to meet more people, fill her hours after work, so she could stop obsessing over her explorer...

Nothing so far had worked, but she'd keep trying. Hopefully, sometime soon, she'd stop crying herself to sleep.

À coeur vaillant rien d'impossible. With enough courage, she could do anything. She was holding on to the thought with everything she had.

Tonight was the first of her cooking classes. The school was a few blocks away, and Rheo would walk around-Prospect Park to get there. She was never going to be a gym bunny, but walking, just getting her blood pumping, made her feel a little closer to Fletch. She would never do a twenty-five-mile hike, or even a three-mile run again, but she didn't need to be a slug.

Rheo tied her shoelaces, put her phone into the back pocket of her jeans, and tucked a twenty-dollar bill into her front pocket, along with the key to her apartment. She jogged down the steps to the lobby and walked out into the late-summer air. Autumn was on its way; the air had turned crisp. Rheo wondered if the leaves were turning in Gilmartin. It was a bit early, but it would happen soon. She missed that little town—something she never thought she'd do.

Rheo hit the sidewalk and waved to Mrs. Bukowski standing at the window of her ground-floor apartment, leaning on her walking sticks. Maybe if it wasn't too late when she got home, she would pop in to see her...

Ooof! Rheo bounced off a hard chest and stumbled backward. A strong hand gripped her arm, and she instantly recognized Fletch's touch. Her eyes slammed into his, and she placed a hand on her heart, scared it would jump out of her chest.

Fletch was *here*. In her city. A place he hated.

"Hello."

His voice sounded deeper, his burr more pronounced. The shock of his arrival closed her throat, and Rheo couldn't get any words out of her mouth. She placed her hand on his chest, needing an anchor.

Fletch was the best there was.

He was here. What the *hell*?

Fletch bent his knees so his eyes—his fabulous eyes she'd missed so much and loved even more—were level with hers.

"Breathe, Rhee."

How could she breathe when he'd flipped her world upside down and inside out? How could he expect that? Rheo grabbed his shirt and twisted her fist to keep him in place. She didn't want him to disappear again.

"Fletch?" she murmured. Then, because she couldn't help it and was so damn tired of missing him, she burst into tears.

Fletch, because he was Fletch, simply pulled her in, gathered her close, and let her cry.

Rheo registered his lips in her hair, his arms around her, and despite everything that had happened, she knew she was where she belonged. Secure, loved. Cherished.

After a few minutes, Fletch stepped back and, using both his thumbs, wiped away her tears. He dropped a soft kiss on her mouth and pulled back to look at her, his eyes soft. "Okay?"

"Now you're here, yes," she told him. "But why *are* you here, Fletch?"

Fletch walked around her small apartment, looking at the black-and-white photographs hanging on her colorful walls. He picked up her hand-blown glass bowl, then the wooden statue of a couple kissing.

How strange, he seemed nervous. She'd never seen him so antsy before.

He walked over to the window, looked out onto her busy street, and turned to face her, his hands gripping the window-sill behind him with white fingers. Definitely uneasy. Why?

"Can I make you some coffee?" she asked, a little anxious herself. But then, anyone would be when the love of their life abruptly walked back in without any warning.

"Coffee is the last thing on my mind," Fletch told her, and wiped his hands on his thighs. Fletch was definitely, and uncharacteristically, nervous.

She looked down at her hand, surprised to see she wasn't shaking. It was enough that he was here. But why was he here?

Rheo sat on the edge of her cream-colored couch and gestured for Fletch to sit opposite her, on her scarlet-and-cream-striped chair. He declined, and she watched him pace the small area in front of the window. Fletch found it difficult to stay still at the best of times, he would have to keep moving to talk. Pity her sitting room was so small…

It was perfect for one person, but when you added a tall muscled man, the space seemed to contract.

"I'm sorry," Fletch said, sounding terse and abrupt. Rheo didn't take offense, she understood his levels of discomfort, and who liked apologizing?

"What are you sorry for, Fletch?"

"For the way I handled the situation in Gilmartin. For the way I handled you."

Rheo thought about protesting. She wasn't a woman who could be handled. But decided there were more important issues at stake than semantics.

"Okay," she replied, waiting for him to explain. When he didn't, she leaned forward and spread her hands. "I'm not sure a quick 'I'm sorry' was worth flying in from wherever you came from…"

"Kentucky." Fletch raked his hand through his hair and she noticed his trembling fingers. It was the strangest thing— the more nervous he appeared, the calmer she became.

"Talk to me, Fletch," she encouraged, fighting the urge to go to him and put him out of his misery. But there was a future to be fought for. If she went to him now, his words might go unsaid.

"I don't know how we can make it work," he stated, his voice low, but full of passion, "but I want to make it work. I *need* to make us work."

And there it was, the words she so desperately wanted to hear.

"But I don't know if it can, *how* it can, without one of us making massive compromises that'll change the essence of who we are together. And if we change the essence of who we are, then we'll change what we love about each other. And then we won't love each other the same way we do now and, God, I don't *fucking know what to do*. I *always* know what to do."

"Fletch?" When his eyes met hers, Rheo told him to breathe. "And another, in and out. Stop panicking."

Fletch stared at her, offended. "I never panic, you can ask my crew. I'm the calmest, most level-headed bloke they know."

Sure, except when he was talking about love and their future, and how they could be together.

"Fletch, come and sit," she told him.

When he reluctantly sat on the chair, Rheo moved to perch on her wooden coffee table, her knees between his. She placed her hands on his thighs, trying not to smile when his grip on the arms of the chair tightened.

"What do you think will happen if you tell me you love me?" she asked. "Do you expect me to demand a ring? A house? A nine-to-five life?"

Panic flared in his eyes. Bingo. So, marriage and commitment didn't scare him, but giving up his career did. She didn't blame him; she didn't want to give hers up either.

"I'd never ask you to stop exploring or stay at home for me, Fletch."

It would be like trying to domesticate a wolf, and they'd both be miserable.

"But how can we be together if we're always so far apart?" Fletch asked her. "It's no basis to build a life on, Rheo."

She tipped her head to the side. "Do you love me, Fletch?"

If he loved her as much as she loved him, then anything was possible.

Emotion rippled through him. "I do. So damn much. I've never loved anyone as much as I do you."

Her heart fluttered in her chest and peace ran through her. She was home, at the place she always longed to be.

"I love you too. And we can figure this out, together."

Hope skittered across his face, and the grip on his arms of the chair loosened. "How?" he demanded.

"I'm not sure yet, Fletch. It's something we need to talk about, discuss, probably argue about." She saw he needed more and shrugged. "Maybe you can shorten your expeditions, or maybe you can accept that offer to present the documentaries of those Lazarus animals, the ones back from extinction? Or maybe you can hack through a thinner jungle or cross a smaller desert." His mouth quirked as hope and humor slipped into his eyes. "Whatever you do, we can be together when you aren't exploring."

"Okay, I can do that. The Lazarus documentaries, that is." He grinned. "I'm hot shit, but I'm not sure I can change the jungles or make the deserts smaller."

She made a show of rolling her eyes before laughing. Then another thought occurred, and she grimaced. "Is there any way you could move your home base to the East Coast so I could keep working at the UN?"

He stroked her arm, from her shoulder to her wrist. "Most

of the planning could be done via video conferencing," he assured her.

"And your production company?"

"The same," he replied. "Being based here wouldn't be a problem."

Rheo knew something was worrying him. She couldn't dive into happiness and excitement until they settled the big issues between them.

"What's still bothering you, Fletch?"

He winced. "I don't think I can live in Brooklyn, Rhee," he admitted. "I'm happy to move closer to you, but I can't do a city."

Fair enough. Rheo thought for a minute. He'd made some pretty big compromises so far. It was her turn to go all in.

"If we were wealthy, I'd suggest we buy a second home, somewhere close enough for me to commute when you are home, but rural enough for you to breathe freely. I could stay here in this apartment when you were away."

Fletch's eyes lightened. "Maybe we don't need a second home. Maybe we only need to buy some land," he told her.

Rheo loved hearing his "we's" and rejoiced at him treating them as a team.

"How so?"

"Despite you raising your pretty little nose at my having a tiny house, it is transportable, and it isn't as tiny as you think. It's probably as big as this apartment. And we could add to it, or build another house, when we have cash, making it bigger and more permanent."

She'd totally forgotten he owned a house, tiny or otherwise. And, frankly, at this point, she'd move into a shed if it meant being with him. Crucially, what they now had were options. Her mind started working overtime.

"We need to find a place, or town, where you feel comfortable, somewhere you are happy to be when you're home," Rheo said, making mental checklists.

"I'm happy wherever you are."

So sweet, but they had a million things to do. Plans to make. She needed a new spreadsheet... "We need to look at our schedules, check real estate listings, we need to—"

Fletch leaned forward and captured her face in his hands. "The only thing I need is for you to tell me you love me. And that we're heading for bed."

Rheo, her lists forgotten, smiled at him, feeling happy and soft. Safe and secure. And horny.

"I love you, Fletcher. Please take me to bed."

Fletch stood, bent his knees, scooped her, and held her against his chest. When their eyes connected, Rheo swallowed at the depth of emotion in his eyes.

"You are, and always will be, my base camp, Rhee."

"And loving you is all the adventure I need, Fletch."

★ ★ ★ ★ ★